The
PARISH
Is the Issue

What I Learned and How I Learned It

LOREN B. MEAD

Morehouse Publishing
NEW YORK

Unless otherwise noted, the Scripture quotations contained herein are from the New Revised Standard Version Bible, copyright © 1989 by the Division of Christian Education of the National Council of Churches of Christ in the U.S.A. Used by permission. All rights reserved.

Morehouse Publishing, 19 East 34th Street, New York, NY 10016

Morehouse Publishing is an imprint of Church Publishing Incorporated.

www.churchpublishing.org

Cover design by Laurie Klein Westhafer
Typeset by Denise Hoff

Library of Congress Cataloging-in-Publication Data

Mead, Loren B.
    The parish is the issue : what I learned and how I learned it / Loren B. Mead.
        pages cm
    Includes bibliographical references.
        ISBN 978-0-8192-3232-8 (pbk.)—ISBN 978-0-8192-3233-5 (ebook)
1. Church. I. Title.
BV600.3.M39 2015
250—dc23
                                                    2015014408

Printed in the United States of America

Contents

Preface

This book is about parishes.

It makes no effort to be objective—it is deeply subjective, probably just as deeply biased. It is written by someone who is into his ninth decade of personal engagement with and membership in a parish and who has worked for six decades professionally in the world of religious organizational life.

A word to the skeptical. This is an important issue that gets little serious attention in our skeptical age.

Reuel Howe, a remarkable scholar from a previous generation, spoke of that larger perspective in 1972:

> Men [that's how we spoke in that generation] have always congregated and always will. Our world will change; the form of the Church will probably change; but because of our nature—especially our dependence upon relationships—we will continue to seek each other out in order to be together. Congregating is a response to a need in ourselves and others and to the presence of something beyond us—the ultimate that speaks to us in all relationships.[1]

I added my own two bits when I stated then what I still believe more than forty years later:

> I happen to believe that the local religious congregation is by far the most important social institution in the world with the possible single exception of the family.[2]

Reuel Howe talks about how "congregating" is a human reality since forever. I assert that congregations are as important as our very families (so important that I've worked with, studied, and wrestled them for over half a century). I believe both these observations to be true, but I suspect you will think I am exaggerating. These views are not very common in the world of 2015, when I am writing this.

So let me invite you on a journey. Give me the benefit of the doubt, and give me also your imagination. What I have to say doesn't fit ordinary conversation or thinking; it will push us beyond simple linear thinking. This journey is not an ordinary journey.

You see, sixty years ago I was a parish pastor in a small church in Berkeley County, South Carolina, a place some people called "Hell Hole Swamp." One of the young people in that parish was a young man named Pard Walsh. Pard grew up there (I married him to Marcy), he became a doctor in Charleston, and is now retired down there. One thing he has done in retirement is take up photography, and a second thing he's done is learn to fly drone aircraft. Right now he is trying to photograph all of "Hell Hole Swamp" and Berkeley County from his drones. He and I are learning all sorts of things we never knew before. How the waterways of that area determine how people get around. How much goes on that you never see when you're just walking around and looking.

Now I'm inviting you to join me on a journey, as if we were in one of Pard's drones. Not a journey through Berkeley County, but one through the world of parishes and family, of churches and religious institutions, looking at all that's been changing and all that goes on when you look really hard.

As I describe this journey, let me be clear—I am seeing things now I did not see all those years ago. I am a different person than I was then. Most significantly, perhaps, during almost all of the journey we will take, I was accompanied by a remarkable woman. Polly. For sixty-three years she graced my life, giving lots of her beauty and her smarts to the four children she gave me and the world. Beauty that was passed on to a flock of grandkids and a smaller flock of great-grandkids. But more than beauty. You see that quote from Reuel Howe? She wrote it. You see, to get me through seminary she worked as a secretary, and as she used to tell me, "I wrote all Reuel's books." She did. Hell. She taught me his theology, and most of the theology that got me through my years of preaching. I'm still pissed that she up and died on me about two years ago, and life isn't nearly as much fun any more.

But on this trip you and I will take through these years of the twentieth and early twenty-first centuries, we'll be concentrating mostly on the professional stuff I worked at as I tried to understand what congregations are and what they are called to become. We'll focus on Reuel's comment about congregating more than on mine comparing the importance of the institution of parishes with the institution of the family. But, remember this, whatever I did was grounded in my relationship with Polly and nurtured by a continuing presence in the living, worshiping soil of a congregation of God's people. Those have been the two groundings of my life.

I have learned a lot in this journey, and I have tried to be honest in what I've told. As honest as I could be, although I admit I do shave the truth occasionally. Some of you will be pleased that I left out some of the dumb things you did; others, angry because I gave my version of stuff you remember differently.

Just remember, every Tuesday morning when I celebrate the Eucharist with the "Tuesday Morning Faithful" at St. Alban's Church, I am careful to say the general confession, remembering it all.

And every night, my prayer is the classic one: "Jesus Christ, Son of God, Have mercy on me, a sinner."[3]

Acknowledgments

Several people, some named in the course of this book, were essential to the work itself and to the articulation of it in these pages—five professional colleagues, one special friend, and a remarkable editorial craftsman: Roy Oswald, Speed Leas, Celia Hahn, Ed White, and Leslie Buhler carried the load with me. Wilma Swanson helped me get started when it all seemed impossible. Richard Bass was the one who held my hand when I started writing this book, refused to let me do too many dumb things, and helped me turn my story into something I hope you find leads you to better ministry where you are.

Loren B. Mead
Eastertide, 2015

PART 1

THE REAL CHURCH IS THE LOCAL CHURCH

CHAPTER 1

To and Through Pinopolis

The *real* church is the local church. I don't know where I got that idea, but I've never been able to shake it.

That place, those people you get together with on Sunday, that's what I mean about "real"—it is that tangible. That simple. Also, that preposterous.

Growing up white and Southern meant that that kind of church was a normal piece of the furniture of my life. Everybody I knew had a church. They were different, those churches, and most of them made jokes about the churches others had. I never really knew there were Jews until I was in high school. I knew there were Catholics, but I didn't know what that meant—I only knew they went to the place at the corner of Irby and Palmetto Streets.

Mother was the serious Christian in the family, and our brand was Episcopalian. Dad wrote checks and came on Easter, but Mother pushed and prodded my brother and me to Sunday school. Dad never took the institutional part of it seriously and wasn't officially a member for a long time—as a matter of fact it was years later, when he and I were talking about what I wanted to be when I grew up and I embarrassedly admitted that I'd occasionally thought about going into the ministry, that he made some shifts. He actually went to confirmation class, was confirmed, and ended up doing all the things a man like him could do: usher, vestryman, senior warden, lay reader. The whole ball of wax. I got the feeling that he hadn't thought much about it until he heard what I'd said. Apparently what I said meant something to him.

Church was, as I said, just part of the furniture of life. Like school, playing football on Saturdays with friends in our yard, the Pecan Bowl. Exhaustive reading at the local library. And organizational leadership—student council, officer of the youth group, head of the parish acolytes (we were trained by my uncle Ben when he came back from World War II). I was on all the responsible committees and participated in the "right" causes—collecting money for good things, collecting scrap iron and toothpaste tubes for the war effort. Trying to be decent to people who were unpleasant or smelled bad.

It's just what you did in South Carolina when you were my age. And you went into the woods and shot things with a .22—mostly cans and bottles, and at Christmas shooting down mistletoe from the trees for decorations. Occasionally going hunting for birds or squirrels. Guns were also just part of our furniture. I never shot anything big, like a deer. Tried, but failed. I was pretty good at "birds," what we called quail. They took shotguns. I never was able to hit doves, but tried that several times too.

The church was where you met your friends. Other friends were in other churches, and it didn't make much difference—we just rarely saw them on Sunday mornings. Sunday evenings we did—evenings were ecumenical. My future wife, Polly, said that in Marion, where she lived, what church you went to all depended on where the best dancers went to youth group.

The theology we lived with was pretty pan-Christian and not very heavy. We knew Bible stories, often told with fundamentalist leanings since most of our friends were Baptist, Methodist, or Presbyterian. Most of the pastors we knew were, like our rector, sweet men, who seemed unrelated to anything we knew. Several were widely disliked—like the Presbyterian guy who seemed to have a grudge against the Catholics, and we had friends who were Catholic. He got bad press from many of us when he took off on something about the Catholics in a baccalaureate sermon one year.

I knew we were Episcopalians because we had a special chair in the church for the bishop. Nobody else sat in it. I knew he was important because whenever he came we had special refreshments after church.

For all of us the local church was what there was. It was there. It was sort of ground zero for what we understood life was all about. And, to tell the truth, it was pretty inconsequential to many of us.

What it did, however, was help us focus on our own lives—our hopes and fears. We really *prayed* about things that bothered us. I mean we had—individually, though not in groups very much—intense dialogue with whatever we'd come to consider God. Dialogue about things we felt guilty about; things we were scared about; things we wanted desperately *not* to get caught about; things we just *had* to have; jams we needed to get out of. Usually nothing global—just stuff we had around us in life. When things turned out OK, we figured somehow God might have been involved. When they didn't turn our OK, we didn't tend to hold a grudge, we just figured "that's how the cookie crumbles."

In words I later learned in sociology—our world was local, not cosmopolitan. Our theology was not systematic, it was situational; it wasn't rational, it was emotional.

But it was real and it was church for us. It was what faith meant to us. I may have, in later years, added a lot of frills to the mix and picked up more sophisticated language and concepts. I'm not sure, though, that I've moved very far from that original church—the one on Dargan Street, the one with the dark wood and high-pitched rafters, the one with the Victorian stained-glass windows, the one where I always sat halfway back on the left-hand side, comforted by seeing the back of Mamie Porter's head a couple of rows ahead of me, seeing the Darbys up on the right in the second pew, Mrs. Griffith on the organ bench. The crowd from Mars Bluff often making up the choir. That beautiful soprano: She was so good she sang solos; so good she could be in the choir even if she was divorced. That was church for me.

Preparing for Formal Ministry

There was more, of course.

At home, my two Catholic cousins (sweet Dottie and Cynthia, who was the baby sister I never had) moved in with us in the forties. Uncle Ben came back from the war to stay at our house too. Dottie and Cynth's mother had died. She was my mother's sister, so both girls came to live with us.

During the war I got out of town each summer—because of the war, resort hotels couldn't get college students as bell hops, so I spent four summers in Cashiers, North Carolina, working at High

Hampton Inn. While there I went to the little ramshackled mission church across the road. It was there, so I went. That's what you did on Sundays. As a matter of fact I went over on VJ Day and rang the church bell.[1]

I fell in love with the mountains in those summers, so I decided to go to college in the mountains too. Sewanee was an Episcopal college, on the Cumberland Plateau in Tennessee. But I went there because it was in the mountains. Not because of academics or church—it was just what you did.

Those were the years of falling into and out of love, or lust, or whatever else was bubbling at the time—but I hit the wall, permanently, at eighteen. When I found Polly, or she found me, everything changed. I cut college a year short and did a quick and dirty master's degree at the University of South Carolina so I could get a job and get married when she graduated in 1951. Problem? She was a Presbyterian, and church had become pretty important to me. Turned out to be no problem. She fell in love with Anglican stuff—the prayer book, the literature of England, and me. So we ended up—me as teacher, she as secretary to head of school—married, Episcopal style, in the same church I was baptized in. And would later be ordained in. I was twenty-one, she was twenty. We settled in Columbia, and our first child arrived almost immediately (nine months and seventeen days later—and both sets of parents counted in those days. Shoot. Back then *everybody* counted.) He was baptized in the same parish we'd been married in before I was ordained there.

I'd found my way as a teacher at the Opportunity School run by Miss Wil Lou Gray, a pioneer in adult education. She was a South Carolina character, known all over for her passion for educating the school dropouts, of which South Carolina was jammed full. Her ideas of education were, well, advanced. She believed the dropout students should study Rome and Athens, but they also ought to visit the places as they studied them. After the war she told her friends in South Carolina (who included Jimmy Byrnes, then secretary of state) she was going to Washington to ask for a surplus, decommissioned battleship to take her students around the world. Her friends knew better than to try to dissuade her, so they sent her off on the train to Washington with fried chicken, sandwiches, and cold drinks. When she came back a week or so later, they greeted her and asked how the trip had gone. "Did you get the battleship?" they asked with barely hidden smirks.

"No." she said. "You know those people in Washington. They don't have any imagination. But they did give me an airport they didn't need any more!" They did—Columbia Army Air Base, 1,000 acres just outside the state capitol (it ended up as the campus of the Opportunity School, of the Area Trade School, *and* the commercial Columbia Airport).

Ever since, I have been careful not to scoff at friends who go off with crazy expectations.

Ministry was still on my mind, but pushed way back, partly for uncertainty, partly for hormones. But it grew stronger over the two years of getting to know the lives of the adult students I was teaching. I discovered they needed much more than English literature to get through life, and I suspected that religious faith might be part of it.

Polly and I went to the Episcopal cathedral in Columbia, but it was really just a parish church. While teaching, I had had two years for voracious reading—much, much history (I remember enjoying even Gibbon! And Benvenuto Cellini and Winston Churchill), but no theology I can remember. I had to push the edges of the deep things in life too. One of my teaching colleagues committed suicide and it fell to me to manage things I had not dealt with—cutting a body down, managing a distraught family, organizing a funeral.

In 1952, though, we headed off to seminary in Virginia. The major influences there were Reuel Howe in pastoral theology, Clinical Pastoral Education at St. Elizabeth's Hospital in Washington, fellow students (ten of us formed our own senior seminar to deal with stuff that wasn't on the seminary's agenda), and a two-year, five-couple group through which we introduced our spouses to the experiential learning we'd discovered in CPE. That group tested us all in group therapy.

I'd always done well in academics, so I did well at seminary, but I did not fall in love with theology. Biblical studies, yes, and even more, studies in pastoral care. Seminary was something I had to do before I could go back to try to lead a local church.

Parish Ministry in South Carolina

Dean Zabriskie at the seminary knew everybody and every place in The Episcopal Church. H shouted across the campus to me in the final months of my seminary experience: "Loren, do you know where the bishop is going to send you yet?"

"Yep," I replied. "He's sending me to Pinopolis. He says it's a growing industrial area just outside Charleston."

"Oh, yeah," Zab replied. "That's 'Hell Hole Swamp,'" he added, apparently trying to be helpful. It wasn't. As a matter of fact, it led me to have a healthy distrust of what bishops would tell me henceforth.

Actually it *was* in Hell Hole Swamp—the coastal area below the Santee River, in the middle of the area in which great plantations had grown the indigo and rice that made pre–Civil War South Carolina both very, very prosperous, and also the center of the slave economy. This country, before the Civil War, had been the center of slavery in the state.[2]

During Prohibition, the area was also famous as a landing place for illegal imports of prohibited liquid goods from the Caribbean, and for some gang warfare about all that. In a New Deal hydroelectric project, the plantations had been flooded, and the plantation owners had moved to the high ground of Pinopolis.[3]

When I checked with the South Carolina State Department of Development for further information, I discovered that in spite of what the bishop had told me, the entire county in which Pinopolis was located (Berkeley County), which had some 30,000 inhabitants, had a total of *three* who were engaged in what the county described as "industry." You now know more of why I take the words of bishops with a grain of salt.

So I walked into my parish, settling into my first house with a wife who was expecting our third child to go with our now two boys. With academic honors and a seminary degree, I was just a small-town boy in a totally alien environment, knowing absolutely nothing about life as a parish pastor. I was broke, so I had to start work even before I could get ordained. I *knew* a lot of theology (Tillich, two Niebuhrs, a literary critical knowledge of the Scriptures, and all that). But I didn't know what I was supposed to do, or when or how to do it.

This was about eight months after the Supreme Court ruled for the desegregation of the schools, and we at seminary had spent energy and time—lots of both—worrying about how this might impact our work, we who were going to parishes in the "rural deep South." Panic was close to the surface for most of us as we read daily newspaper accounts that talked of "massive resistance" and "nullification," and our kinfolk told us how angry everyone was. We heard about how upset people were at "outside agitators." We wondered if we were going to be perceived as such agitators. When one of my best friends at seminary joined the NAACP, I thought he was crazy, but I envied his craziness. No other white person I'd ever known would have done that.

I walked into the beautiful white building that was to be my church, my primary center of ministry. It was absolutely beautiful, with clear glass windows and a magnificent clear fan window above the altar, looking out on massive long-leaf pines in what I would soon find out was Doc Fishburne's yard. I loved its brightness, its white paint, the colonial box pews. Outside was an enormous magnolia tree, and crepe myrtles lined the one dirt road through town. There was a one-room post office across that road where I soon learned everybody gathered to talk when the mail came. The setting was straight from an eighteenth-century novel, only American. I looked around the church where I was to learn to preach. There was a processional cross and a flag. I felt immediately at home.

Oh my God!

It was not the flag I expected—the forty-eight-star, thirteen-stripe Old Glory I'd found in many churches during World War II. It was a Confederate Stars and Bars flag!

It knocked me for a loop. What should I do? I didn't know much, but with all the baggage I'd brought with me from seminary—long conversations about the growing tensions over race, the arguments in local papers and on the radio, I knew two contradictory things. I *knew* the flag had to go. I couldn't stand what it stood for. I knew just taking it out all by myself would violate all sorts of relationships as well as any sense of commonality with the parish leadership. A clear no-win situation. Who should I ask? The bishop had assigned a clergy mentor for me, but I already knew he was an alcoholic and undependable. I was alone, I felt. So I did what I felt I *had* to do, knowing it was strategically a very bad step. I moved the flag out by myself, without asking anybody, and I never told anyone what I'd done. (I've wondered since if I really thought nobody would notice! I just did it. I felt I had to!)

Nobody said anything to me about it. Silence. We went three years, doing all sorts of things together—many of them first-rate things. But nobody spoke about what I had done with the flag. Until three years later.

I had already made my decision to leave Pinopolis for a call to Chapel Hill, North Carolina, and I went to see Miss Carrie Cain, the person whose depth of faith and love had sustained me for three years. She had taught me more than I can say—all the things I had not learned at seminary. She not only had become my seminary, she was one of the most extraordinary persons of faith I've ever known. (Years later I dedicated a book, *Transforming Congregations for the Future*, to her.) I told her I was going to leave. She gave me wonderful feedback about my work and the state of the parish, and then she asked me one question. "I need to know," she said, "why you moved our flag." I don't know to this day what I said in reply. I may well have lied to her. At that moment I knew I had missed something important. As I have come to understand it, I had judged their symbol through my prejudice, not theirs. I have tried to hold that learning close to my heart ever since. When I went back to the parish office that day, I looked in the parish register and found dozens of names recorded, including several of her father's generation, with the notation that they were "KIA" in the war that they still called *the* war.

But I've never forgotten it. All of it. It was a turning point inside me.

It was while in Pinopolis that I had a major learning experience in what was called a Group Life Laboratory—basically an introduction to group dynamics and the pedagogy of experiential education. This ten-day conference simply reoriented us to how groups work. It substantially influenced all the teaching I've done since then, as well as my understanding of the way to lead groups and plan change.

Through this period of my work, I think my primary model of what I was doing was based in a therapeutic approach. If something was wrong, that approach assumes it could be fixed, but first you had to understand it. If you understood it, you could figure out how to change it so it would work. Maybe you'd have to tinker with it, but eventually it could be fixed. Then you could tell or teach other people how to diagnose similar problems and fix them. It was a model adapted from the world of medicine (my father was a doctor, so the approach was familiar to me), the presuppositions of the academic world that had trained me for two decades, and the reinforcement of doing clinical pastoral education in the therapeutic setting of a psychiatric hospital. But those presuppositions were beginning to be challenged—by learning about the ambiguities of human life through the world of psychiatry, through intense personal engagements in group therapy, and through what some of us had begun to sense in what we later learned to call family systems thinking—as I struggled with the pastoral care of a flood of alcoholism in my parish. The best "therapy" I could find didn't seem to "fix" very much, or for very long.

With lots of learning under my belt—several disasters, a number of new boundaries crossed, with a pretty chastened picture of what I was able to do as a pastor, but with no little growing commitment to the life of the local congregation—I collected myself for the challenge of a mission church in North Carolina, with perhaps the loudest advice being to "Watch out for all those Communists in Chapel Hill."

CHAPTER 2

From Old South to New South

Pinopolis is the heart of conservative, aristocratic nostalgia for the Old South. The people in the parish were extraordinary individuals, many with impressive depths of spirituality and just sheer knowledge, but the world there faced the past. Chapel Hill carries some of the same history, but had also become part of the New South—brash, loud, "progressive," and packed with intellectual stimulation as well as pretension. It was trying to connect to the future.

From a hunting and fishing paradise of slow-moving living to a pulsing, impatient, future-oriented maelstrom of ideas and issues—that sketches some of the distance between those two worlds. The biggest day of the year in Pinopolis was the day duck season started, although some would say deer season. In Chapel Hill, it was the day of the Duke-Carolina football game. Or the ACC basketball championship.

Local church in Pinopolis was settled, quiet, hereditary, traditionally Anglican—the one significant theologian The Episcopal Church had produced in the nineteenth century, William Porcher Dubose, was known there as "Cud'n Willie." It was a church of "Christendom," a piece of southern Anglican memorabilia.[1] The senior warden of the next-door parish in Eutawville was a magnificent man everyone knew as "Maas Willie Gilliard." The *people* were beginning a wrenching transition to a modern, fast-paced television world, but the church was not. The people were black people and white people.[2] Rigidly separate, black people and white people. Not equal. Intentionally separate, intentionally not equal. Secretly I had already joined the organization

John Morris had started to advocate for racial justice (The Episcopal Society for Cultural and Racial Unity—ESCRU).[3] I joined it secretly because no white man in his right mind in Berkeley County, South Carolina, would have done so publicly. In Pinopolis, ESCRU was subversive; in Chapel Hill, it was a strong option.

The local church I was called to serve was a brand new mission on the edge of Chapel Hill, hometown of the new theologian Urban Tigner Holmes III, who at that very time was writing *The Future Shape of Ministry*.[4] It was a town full of academics, scholars, scientists, thinkers, and planners from all sorts of fields, especially medicine. It was right next to what came to be called Silicon Valley East—the Research Triangle. But that was before Silicon Valley got its name, and the Research Triangle was an idea perched among barren pines of the Piedmont south. The white people and black people were separate, but there was considerable communication. Chapel Hill had a Fellowship for the Integration of the Schools that met in public every month. Met *in public*!

At the new church in Chapel Hill, I was working within church patterns passed on from the rural past of North Carolina's establishment while trying to invent forms and structures for a world in radical transition, one that had no clarity about what needed to change and why or how. There was confidence about what lay ahead in the future, but total confusion about exactly what needed to be done to live into that future.

In my continuing education while in Pinopolis I had heard a theory from Kurt Lewin that I have come to see explains some of my cultural displacement. Lewin (a key early thinker about human relations) asserted that "change" was a complex concept. Every situation we run into is in equilibrium. It is in stasis (sometimes only for a brief time, but stuck in one place), with offsetting and confrontative forces balanced to support its stability. *Some* equilibriums were stable, or even "stuck," over time and very resistant to change.

It was as if things were frozen into immobility. In Pinopolis that equilibrium was frozen in the past age.

Three things, Lewin said, were needed to make change happen: (1) The equilibrium needed to be "unfrozen"; (2) the desired change then had to be installed; and (3) the new situation, with the change in place, needed to be "refrozen."[5]

In Pinopolis there was comfort with that given equilibrium, a stable balance of forces facing the past. In Chapel Hill, I was finding considerable discomfort, if not anger, at the equilibrium we lived in, but passionate disagreement about which direction the equilibrium should be pushed. There were forces looking to the past, but newer and stronger forces were pushing us toward change.

Lewin's theories missed one other ingredient: He did not prepare us for the fact that the world around situations—the environment, the context—might itself be in rapid transition. So the endpoint of the process of change was not to a new stability, but to a world that was already changing from where you started and would continue to be in its own processes of change. (It was Chapel Hill and North Carolina's own novelist Thomas Wolfe who said it in his most famous book: You can't go home again. Home has already moved!)

The cultural world of Chapel Hill was already being unfrozen by social forces far beyond the understanding of most of us. Many in the culture were participating in the unfreezing and were active advocates for change of all sorts. The world of religious institutions was less open to change, based as it was in forms invented and sustained by cultural reinforcement now generations old.

What is new in my thinking now was not fully there then: The whole world was in rapidly escalating change, and the equilibrium we needed to unfreeze needed to be changed to a different order of being—in essence a new *kind* of "stability" that had more capacity for flexibility than the previous state. Comic book ads from the 1930s hailed Charles Atlas's "Dynamic Tension" method of bodybuilding. That phrase—dynamic tension—captures some of what the new state needed to be.

The ideas and thinking that swam around us as we worked on parish life came from people working in the Research Triangle on systems concepts, from people struggling with city and regional planning, from leadership and management problem solvers at the Institute of Government and the University School of Business. Conversations in the parish vestry or in social gatherings brought new thoughts from people working on DNA and RNA. In other words, the world we had moved into was a soup of learning. My own understanding of what I was trying to do as a parish priest got modified by what I was learning about how people organized themselves to accomplish things, how different people comprehended things in different ways, and how congregations interfaced with cultural systems and community life.

Not only that. The social and cultural realities were from another world. I arrived in Chapel Hill to be a parish pastor in December. I began planning my parish program for the spring; in Episcopalian language, that means "Lent," and in those days that meant "study courses." I did not realize that the previous spring, the University basketball team had gone undefeated and had won the NCAA national title. I did not understand that the most important thing—religious or otherwise—in the *world that year* for Chapel Hill people was the basketball season. God was a bit player in that world.

My understanding of what my vocation was, as priest of a parish, had to deal with a new reality. The parish was in a very different world, the people were very different people, and, I guess, I was a different priest. Because the people of my parish were wonderful, understanding, and loyal church people, they actually did come to the meetings I called for study groups, but many of them brought transistor radios on game nights while I gamely taught on about whatever it was we were studying.

In Chapel Hill, I was not in a stable congregation.

Although I was not *in* the future church, I began to realize I was in-between the kind of church I'd grown up in, the church of Pinopolis, and another kind of church that was in its birthing stage all around me. We were in-between.

Without exactly knowing what I was doing, I started edging my way toward that as-yet-undefined church. That's the tension I spoke to in the title and substance of my book, still three decades in the future: I was at the same time in the once and the future church.

I think my first try was to "update" the bylaws that described how the parish worked. I did so, developing a parish structure that was a perfect fit with the structure of the national Episcopal Church. It was consistent with the best thinking of the National Churches of Christ too. Everything fit; it was elegant. It even fit the World Council of Churches. It also wasn't bad in reflecting pretty good management thinking.

But the darned people didn't want to work in the perfect structures I had developed. So my perfect structure didn't accomplish what I designed it to do.

I think it took me three years to realize it didn't work. I'm not always a quick learner, particularly when I'm convinced that my system is perfect. The world kept changing on me. All the other agencies switched their structures and their articulation of what they were about. Now they didn't fit each other *or* us. I was learning the interactive dynamic of the parish. Elegance (even theological elegance) is not enough. A parish is part of a living world, the living organism within which it exists. We needed to be flexible and connected dialogically with the community and world outside our bounds.

Years later I learned how Frank Porter Graham, the president of the University of North Carolina, arranged the walkways on the newly built campus quad. He refused to draw a map of where the brick walkways should be laid out. Instead, he waited through a winter after the buildings had been put in to see where students trampled grass as they went from where they were to where they wanted to be. That's where he had bricklayers construct the walkways. We needed to learn to live that way.

What to do? I didn't know. I took my clue from Senator Patrick Moynihan of New York who, pointing to a tension point in race relations, suggested taking some time to practice "benign neglect" of the structures until we had a better handle on what was going on. So we quietly quit paying much attention to the rules of the organization, deciding to do what needed doing, organizing what needed to be organized to do that—and left the structures be.

I paid my dues—doing what needed doing to build a parish: education, lots of community building and incorporation of new people as they appeared, supporting the diocese. Building on the Pinopolis experience, I spent much time in ministry related to medical and alcoholism issues and family ministry. I started learning how to run an every member pledge campaign to raise money for a budget. I even started learning what a budget *was*. I got better at leading worship with imagination, and I grew from a weak preacher to a middling good one—occasionally pretty darned good.

Growth happened, and within a few years we were "promoted" from a mission church to a full-fledged parish. We were "successful." We thought we were doing it ourselves. We did not realize there was something going on around us that came to be known as the Baby Boom. All over the country all sorts of institutions—businesses, schools, fraternal clubs (as Robert Putnam noted in *Bowling Alone*—even bowling leagues) were being flooded with new members. Members that were easy come, but *also* easy go! I found myself being pulled more and more into trying to understand what a congregation, a parish, really was.

While taking a course at the Institute of Advanced Pastoral Studies in Detroit, I investigated a remarkable institution then on its last legs—Parishfield Community in Brighton, Michigan. The thinking they pioneered among laity and scholars had spun off the Detroit Industrial Mission and related to the larger ecumenical movement: Suzanne de Dietrich's methods for small group study of the Scriptures, Hendrik Kraemer's *Theology of the Laity*, and connections to the World Council of Churches. I discovered a wealth of working papers being developed by people around the world—Paul Van Buren and Gibson Winter (both of Parishfield), who led me to Colin Williams and Tom Wieser and Bill Webber at East Harlem. Many of them began collecting their work through the WCC's Study of the Missionary Structure of the Congregation. Tom Allen and George Macleod in Scotland. Joost de Blank in South Africa. Ernie Southcott from Leeds. I knew them through their books, but even more through the medium of the day—mimeographed papers. Lots of mimeographed papers. Tom Wieser of Geneva put together *The Planning of Mission*. Betty O'Connor began publishing exciting material from the Church of the Savior in Washington, where Gordon and Mary Cosby were working. The National Training Laboratories were flooding the market with new knowledge about organization and management.

In Chapel Hill around this time I had a conversion about what I understood ministry to be about. I'd come out of seminary believing it was primarily a matter of—I'll oversimplify it—personal and spiritual therapy. The pastor and the parish existed primarily to help individuals sort out their lives in relationship to God, discover their own place in God's forgiveness and love, and build or rebuild healthy relationships with their family and community. It was a person-to-person thing that the parish gave space for, and the pastor was the center of pastoral care.

Doing that work made me focus a lot on various ways to enable personal counseling, including family counseling. But one day, working with a parishioner in my office on a troubled marriage issue, I had a sort of out-of-body experience and looked down at the two of us in my office as if from above, and said: "Loren, just what are you up to? This town has more help for this kind of problem than almost any place in the country—a first-class psychiatric center; a couple of dozen really good pastoral counselors and pastors; and a whole department of psychology and school of social work with dozens of pretty good counselors of all sorts—but this town is turning out broken people faster than the whole bunch of us can fix them."

It was a sobering experience. My basic model of what I was about was broken.

The model I had been working with was based on a medical model—bringing healing to those who are in poor health, if not actually sick. It is also the model of much evangelism—bringing the gospel message to the person who does not already "have" it. Within the actual world of medicine, there is another model that is more systemic—that of public health, which works to change the character of the community so that disease-bearing systems are replaced by methods and systems that carry away the pathogens that spread bad health. In a more biblical way of saying it, salvation is not about saving the "soul" but about bringing health and wholeness to the entire person.

Pretty soon that kind of thinking led me to shift my model of what we were up to from the one-on-one therapeutic model to what I came to call the "systems model." Whereas I had thought of the parish as a therapeutic center helping people sort out their lives, I began to see the parish as a system—an interactive community within the town and county whose job was to *be* a center of health and forgiveness in the midst of a death-dealing social system. We needed to be a community whose health was contagiously related to the social ills of the outside world, a place where individuals would be surrounded by a community that helped them find and "catch" wholeness, not disease. Bodily *and* spiritually.[6] Jesus put it as "abundant life."

Systems language began to come naturally to me—many people I worked with used systems categories at the Research Triangle Institute. I had also begun to use Rolf Lynton[7] as an informal parish consultant, which started when he helped me design and carry out a parish vestry weekend, and I found out what a consultant could do to help make things happen. He put me onto the thinking of others in management and training who worked from a systems perspective and wrote about it. His book *Training for Development,*[8] together with other writings from members of the National Training Laboratories, pushed my thinking.

Over the next decade the parish and I engaged in a number of areas, some of them distinct and different, others intertwined with what was the ordinary work of the parish and my increasing responsibilities in the diocese. All of them tended to push me further toward understanding the parish as a system within the larger system of the community—working to strengthen the forces of wholeness in all the systems we touched. Moving from a person-to-person focus to a systems focus was difficult. Traditional parish structures were not sensitized to that approach to their tasks.

CHAPTER 3

Race, Parish, and Community

The path to learning about the church was not neat in my experience. As I reflect on it and try to recapture the learning curve, it was not singular and unified. It was not planned. Things happened and I responded. Sometimes I was a bystander watching what happened. Sometimes I initiated or pushed. I was deeply engaged in four themes that occurred simultaneously, often influencing each other.

These are the tracks I worked with as I look back over those years: (1) racial relations and their impact on parish issues; (2) interchurch planning and the Industrial Mission; (3) liturgy and parish systems; and (4) missions and mission research.

In December 1957, when I joined the story at Chapel Hill, the Church of the Holy Family was a church with white members in a Southern town with traditional, segregated systems. Chapel Hill was not really Old South; there was a seething undercurrent of resentment about all sorts of issues, with race being perhaps the most urgently felt by many. A group of liberal people was vocal and had organized to try to desegregate the schools. There was also a very bitter, but often silent, group passionately ready to defend the status quo. For most Southerners like me, it was surprising to be exposed to the passionate liberal voices—in my experience, nobody much had been a voice for change. We were generally warned against those who were for any kind of change.

We were not surprised when our next-door neighbor in Chapel Hill, a wife of a professor in the Department of Philosophy, published a bitter paperback, *Blood on the Old Well*, cataloguing the "sins"

20

attributed to the liberals in Chapel Hill. And the airwaves across the state featured an every-night barrage of right-wing radio from soon-to-be senator Jesse Helms in Raleigh.

I got involved myself when I was asked to serve on a committee working to help those with low income and poor jobs—mostly in the black community between Chapel Hill and Carrboro. The committee was part of a statewide effort: It was one of the first "Grey Area" programs sponsored by the Ford Foundation. We did not know at the time that this was a model effort to get people out of poverty. It later became a forerunner of Lyndon Johnson's War on Poverty.

From my point of view it also got me personally connected to some black people in the town, in particular to Howard Lee, who was a PhD student at the University, and to several black clergy. We worked on several issues, and I remember learning how so many of the people in poverty were working hard at jobs, sometimes multiple jobs, and had terrible issues with finding childcare while they worked.

But it was in the ministerial association that we first ran into the issue of access to community resources, the complex set of issues that really woke up the civil rights movement. The local movie theater, which was segregated, booked the new production of *Porgy and Bess*, featuring well-known black actors and actresses. In the local press it was pretty widely praised. Several students at the black high school asked their teacher to try to arrange for them to see the film—perhaps a special showing, since blacks were not allowed to attend regular showings. She took the request to her minister, whose request was turned down by the theater manager. Her minister then brought the request to the ministerial association for help. We had no idea what to do, so we sent a couple of the white ministers to make the request again, hoping that would work.

When that was also refused, and negotiations were blocked, we encouraged each other to talk to our church members about not going to the theater during the showing of *Porgy and Bess*. I don't think we had any idea of what was going on. We did not know what "boycott" meant. The Greensboro sit-ins were several weeks in the future. We just thought the black kids ought to be able to see the black actors and actresses. If it *was* a boycott we started, it was pretty poorly organized or thought out. My kids, Polly, and I joined the movement, so none of us saw movies for a while. It was just fifty miles away a few weeks later that students in Greensboro did the first sit-in at the drug store lunch counter.

About then Howard Lee's professor asked him to "house sit" his home while he and his family spent the summer in Massachusetts. Howard was delighted, but the professor's neighbors were not—and his professor lived in our neighborhood. Robert Seymour (a remarkable Southern Baptist pastor), several other pastors, and I did some quick and dirty home visits to help open the doors of the neighborhood. It worked well, and Howard's family was welcomed.

Another nearby neighborhood, which had a co-op dues-paying swimming pool to which my family belonged, ran into a similar issue— one of the families seeking membership in the pool had adopted children of other races—and the co-op board rejected their membership. My own children, and those of some others, agreed that was not fair— so we, and others, resigned our memberships.

We were not trying to "start something" in either of these cases. It just seemed unfair. And, to be honest, my kids and I did not appreciate staying out of the swimming pool in the summer in Chapel Hill. It was hot!

The issues moved downtown to public access to eating places and other public segregated areas. The bus station. Mayor Sandy McClamroch, a member of my parish, got the city council to empanel the Mayor's Committee on Human Relations to help handle what was going on. Several protest marches were held, but each was carefully done, with nonviolence training for the participants. What was happening in our town began to be influenced by activities we saw nightly on television. My connections to the meetings on poverty in Carrboro and my role in the minister's association put me in the middle of the emerging protests. Protest marches began, and I participated. Sandy asked me to chair the new committee, and I agreed.

Things got tense. We edged toward open conflict. People got scared.

Our parish was not unanimous in support of what was going on, and I think my public role was difficult for some parish members to be happy with, but I also had substantial support, and I was aware that many of my colleagues in Southern churches did not have that support.[1]

One area with direct impact on the parish was our decision to host an interracial Vacation Bible School during the summer. Many of us felt it important that our children have more chances to meet children of other races before the approaching school integration, and having an interchurch, interracial Vacation Bible School seemed a good step. Because our church and its playground was right on the highway bypass, the initiative was very visible. I remember one anxious mother, who asked her son how the first day had gone, was both perplexed and happy when he said, "It was great. Good classes. We had races and games. Good Kool-Aid." When she persisted, still anxious, she asked, "Were there any Negroes in your class?" "I don't know," he answered, "I'll ask my teacher tomorrow!"

That summer, pressure mounted and protests multiplied, mostly over allowing black citizens access to eating and shopping areas previously closed to them. I began a summer of involvement that was hectic for several reasons: (1) Much of my work for the mayor involved three-way negotiations between the protesters, the police department, and the merchants' association—all of whom had critical roles in keeping peace in the town and all of whom had different stakes in the protests; (2) most of the merchants' association members went on vacation in August, at the peak of the heat and the controversy, so it was hard to connect with them at the most difficult times; (3) the protestors, many of them students at the University and in the black public schools, tended to begin their planning meetings near midnight; and (4) I had a parish to run, with people getting married and dying, and with early morning services several times a week.[2]

Two other things happened that deepened my involvement with the racial tensions around the parish and community. First came a phone call from a member of the vestry—a doctor in the pathology department of the hospital. "Loren," he began, "I just hired a new cytology technologist for my lab." "Uh huh," I replied. "She says she's interested in The Episcopal Church. Her husband is in service overseas and he's an Episcopalian," he continued. "What's the problem?" I asked. "She's black," he said. A lot went through my head. The parish *was* all white. There were a number of people clearly not ready to welcome a black member. I remembered that the annual financial campaign was the next month, and this just seemed the wrong time for me to face this. I didn't want anything to get in the way of making the budget! I was ashamed of thinking like that; indeed, now more than half a century later, I am ashamed that that was what popped into my head.

"George," I continued, trying to hide my anxiety, "What would you do for anybody else who told you he or she wanted to come to our church?" I knew George, and I knew what he would say. He did. "I'd invite her to come to church with me Sunday!" "Then what's the problem?" I asked, knowing in my guts that there was a problem. "Well, I wanted to check it out with you," he said.

I called a couple in the parish I knew would welcome the young woman heartily. Then I made sure the ushers would not be surprised and would sit her by the couple I had alerted. There were no glitches, and when the young woman came, she enjoyed the morning, and soon became a strong and dedicated member of the parish. When her husband came back from overseas, he joined her, and the two of them soon had a lovely daughter who was baptized in the church.

The second event was my discovery of a piece of hidden reality I ran into that pushed me, personally, to a new level of my understanding. The diocesan Department of Christian Social Relations had begun meeting at our church, which was near the center of the diocese. One member was a splendid layman, John Sullivan, who drove to the meetings from his home in Charlotte. At one of our first meetings, when we broke for lunch, the members split up among several cars to drive to a nearby café where I'd discovered racially mixed groups could eat together. I chose to ride with John, and was allocated to the backseat of his car. Getting in, I stumbled over something on the floor—it turned out to be a large empty coffee can.

"What is this?" I asked, rather oblivious to the facts.

"Oh," said John, "It's a long way from Charlotte, and I'm not sure if it's safe to stop many places if I need to take a leak."

That simple fact blew me over. I simply had not recognized the personal costs—really not enormous, but mind-boggling to me—that a black man paid, every day, for being black in our society. Something shifted in me that day—racial separation came home to me in a new way.

Meanwhile, as the South experienced controversy, daily reports of racial confrontations, demonstrations, and police reactions appeared on television and in the newspapers. Within The Episcopal Church, ESCRU had become a strong voice, and many clergy and laity found its voice essential and supportive in facing the emerging issues. In addition to bringing support to those in the South open to desegregation, ESCRU brought in people and resources from northern and western states. And across the country it helped countless people like me, struggling to adjust our lives to deeper understandings of dynamics that had been hidden by society under a cloak of silence. That work of opening the door for white people to become active in the civil rights movement was a major accomplishment of ESCRU.

Indeed, John Morris and ESCRU became leaders when the "Freedom Rides" began, eventually sponsoring one bus of freedom riders to Jackson, Mississippi. That particular bus, which included some people I knew, was stopped and some riders were beaten badly. When they got to Jackson, the person who welcomed them in public was Medgar Evers, the head of the NAACP there. Many of the leaders of the white churches there felt they had to keep their distance from them. Evers helped them find housing, medical help, and food, and they were grateful.

A few weeks later, Evers was shot and killed as he returned home from a meeting. His wife, Myrlie, telephoned John Morris to ask if he would invite a group from ESCRU to come to the funeral. When John phoned me to ask me to go, I agreed, and I flew to Jackson and participated in the funeral. I remember it was 110 degrees that day for that long march in the sun in Jackson. There were thousands there, with ten pale, white-faced, somewhat anxious Episcopal clergy somewhere in the middle of the throng. It was also the last time I was with Martin Luther King Jr. (When he had seen us white people in our clerical collars in the coach section of the plane from Atlanta, he had sent us a note: "Glad to see you boys in the back of the bus!")

It was during that long, hot march through Jackson that I experienced a small taste of what many blacks felt then and still feel about the presence of police. White police in riot gear stood all along the route of the procession. I knew from my own experience that they were mostly fine young men, probably sons of farming families from the nearby country—but in their helmets and riot gear they were intimidating to us on the road.

While the ten of us were in Jackson, we took the initiative to ask the local Episcopal clergy to meet with us—it was a classic case of "outside agitators" meeting the local, would you call them, "agitates"? It was a solid, helpful meeting, during which we expressed our support for them in their difficult roles, stated that we understood some of them could not, and possibly did not want to, participate in our march, but that we had felt bound to come. I remain glad that we tried to connect and feel our being there was important for them as well as for us. John Allin, later presiding bishop of The Episcopal Church, was dean of the cathedral there, and he hosted our meeting.

ESCRU was never a large organization, but I think it was enormously important. Many of us had few connections to the protesters, and ESCRU gave us "cover" and made it possible for many of us to come out of this particular closet. ESCRU had done much to get white churchmen engaged in civil rights—from going to Selma to simply beginning to support new racial policies where they lived and went to church. In time the white people among us did what we often do in groups like that—we assumed we were "in charge." I am proud that when that time did come, and blacks and whites recognized what was happening, John and the leaders of ESCRU went out of business in order to support the work of the Union of Black Episcopalians. John Morris never received the recognition for what he did and the role he played.

Shortly after that busy, hot, contentious summer, my family and I went to England in a parish exchange that had been arranged for some time. When I got back, the scene had changed—the public accommodation law was operating, Kennedy had been assassinated, and the public issue had moved from racial integration to the war in Vietnam—as some would have it, another aspect of racism.

CHAPTER 4

Interchurch Relations

More and more our church world in North Carolina had begun thinking regionally, not just locally. Three towns and three counties rubbed elbows, and right smack dab in the middle a new entity had been born. A previous governor of the state, Luther Hodges, had initiated talk and then action to establish what was called the Research Triangle Park—a substantial geographical park between the towns and right next to the Raleigh-Durham airport. Governor Malcolm Seawell and his successors continued to build on that beginning

The dream was that this park could be home to substantial efforts by industry and government to focus research activities, backed up by the resources of the three great universities—The University of North Carolina at Chapel Hill, Duke University in Durham, and North Carolina State University at Raleigh.

I discovered some implications of the developing interrelationships for our parish serendipitously by doing what I did every week, scheduling worship services for my parish. It was Lent, and Episcopalians (and others too, obviously) usually have special services then, especially during Holy Week leading up to Easter. The Sunday I announced my plans for Holy Week services, I was accosted by one of my wardens—Phil McMullan.[1] He asked me, "What are all these services you have scheduled for next week?" as he noted my plans for daily Holy Communion services.

"It's our tradition, Phil," I answered him patiently. (I think I was probably talking down to him, since obviously I had been to seminary and he hadn't.)

"Why is that?" he responded.

"Well, we always have special worship services that week because that was the week Jesus was approaching his crucifixion, and we think we ought to spend some special time thinking about that in prayer."

He shot back: "But all those services are at 7:30 in the morning," he said, "and I have to be on the road to work out at the Triangle by 7:00. That means I, and almost everybody who works where I do, can't get here."

I honestly hadn't thought about that.

Phil went on: "If it's so important, why don't you plan something I *can* get to?"

Stumped, I said, "Well, Phil, our parish does have a half dozen or so who work out there, so I could come out there and have a service at lunchtime if you could find a place."

"Great," he said, "I'll check it out."

After a few calls, we arranged that I'd come out at lunchtime on Wednesday. We'd use a small, unoccupied room, and he would let people know about the service.

I went out that Wednesday and met him where he told me to, and we went in to the room—actually a medium-sized classroom surrounded by green chalkboards. I was expecting the six to eight folks I knew from the parish.

There were over fifty people there, and I didn't know most of them. After I picked up my jaw, we went on with the service, then stood around for a short chat. I discovered that the people there were all sorts of people from all sorts of congregations from Raleigh and Durham and Chapel Hill. Not all of them were Episcopalians, either; but they were all people wanting special religious connection with Jesus's week of trial and crucifixion.

The situation was way ahead of me. Religion and relationships to God and to each other did not fit into my plans for the day. Something was going on that didn't fit the religious structures I had in mind.[2] I was thinking about my parish, about denominations, towns and counties, and apparently God was dealing with another geography.

I started reaching out and tried to see what was happening in other places. I had already located the thinkers and actors at Parishfield, and I soon discovered that in a number of places interdenominational groups were forming to explore and work with the kind of pluriformity I had backed into in my Lenten service. People in the Detroit area had formed the Detroit Industrial Mission. In Los Angeles, there was the Los Angeles Goals Project; in Cincinnati, the Cincinnati Industrial Mission; in Boston, the Boston Industrial Mission; in Philadelphia, MAP or the Metropolitan Associates of Philadelphia. Hartford had a strong and very active group of downtown congregations. And there were many more.

The common theme was that they were people of faith, based in local congregations of various kinds, in interconnected agencies and industries, all trying to enhance the quality of the communities they shared. For many of them, the skills of planning were central. I'd even found people like that in other parts of the Research Triangle.

I began trying to gather local church leaders from Raleigh, Durham, and Chapel Hill to begin working at collaborative approaches to making life better. Because of where we were, there was a lot of concern focused on issues of race and of poverty. But as I got started, I hit an immediate snag. I couldn't get the clergy I knew best—mostly the other local Episcopalians—interested in the idea. I heard that Colin Williams, a key figure in the World Council of Churches' studies on the congregation, was coming to the area to speak at Duke, so I wrote him to see if I could get his advice on how to get regional involvement.

He and I met for breakfast between Durham and Chapel Hill. When I told him about the lack of response, he simply said: "Who did you ask?" When I told him "All the Episcopal clergy I know," he said even more simply: "Is that all there are?"

Of course not. There was Buie Seawell, starting a new Presbyterian church; Don Shriver, who was the Presbyterian chaplain at NC State (and later the author of many books and president of Union Theological Seminary); a trio of extraordinary Baptist clergy; a UCC pastor soon to lead the North Carolina Council of Churches; and a neat Catholic priest who had marched with us for civil rights. A wealth of talent I simply had overlooked, stuck as I was in my denominational straitjacket.

Broadening the base, we very soon had a fascinating conversation going about how the churches might help shape the megacity that was being formed from Raleigh, Durham, and Chapel Hill. Thinking began to gel when we took a two-day retreat together. We started calling ourselves the Triangle Area Task Force.[3] The long-term outcome was that Don Shriver sought and received a small grant from the Babcock Foundation in Winston-Salem, and we put together an

"Industrial Mission" we named Complex, Inc., a coalition of churches, businesses, and individuals. Our goal was to influence, through the processes of the three cities' planning offices and the Research Triangle Institute Planning Office, how the three communities would build the new city. The board was predominately made up of laity engaged in the enterprises of the Triangle. Buie Seawell, pastor of the new Presbyterian Church of Reconciliation and the son of North Carolina's attorney general (a staunch supporter of the Research Triangle), became the executive director and led its efforts until the money ran out, about three years later.

External pressures came from the continuation of the civil rights movement in our area and around the country. Newspapers gave us daily reminders of cities that were experiencing traumatic change—Birmingham, Detroit, Wilmington, Delaware. And local protests about access to public accommodations expanded, with paralysis around eating places and movies.

For a couple of years I audited courses at the University's School of City and Regional Planning, hoping to find expertise in discovering how to make cities more humane. I did not find much help. Complex, Inc., did, however, bring a number of the congregations into conversation about their role in the emerging city. Laypeople discovered people in other organizations who saw the possibilities of better communities. Conversation did not go far, however. Money ran out, and Buie decided to go to law school in Colorado. When I asked him why he was doing that, he told me: "All the work we did in these cities made it clear how hard it is to change things. And that lawyers wrote all the rules about what was allowed to happen. Not only *that*," he added, "but lawyers write all the rules about how to change the rules! So I decided to go to law school!" He went on to do good work in law, politics, and teaching in Colorado.

In all these efforts I felt we were trying to move ministry beyond the therapeutic, person-to-person mode toward looking at systemic effort to affect the quality of community life. When Complex ended, I pushed the board to meet to reflect on what we had learned. At that evaluation meeting, Howard Lee, the young man I had met in the poverty program in Carrboro, showed up, having been on the board of Complex. He said, "Well, we didn't get done all we wanted to do, but all this work sure did get me into politics!" I felt we had moved the image of what lay ministry was all about. One of the last things

I did before leaving Chapel Hill was to go to the public celebration of Howard's election as mayor. Singing "We shall overcome" had powerful meaning that night. Many of us who were there had a real sense that we *had* overcome. We had elected our first nonwhite mayor, we had elected a school board that would begin integrating the schools, and we had done so without demonizing the other side.[4] Not one party had overcome or won, but in a new way the larger community of Chapel Hill had overcome some of its traditional blockages.

CHAPTER 5

Rethinking Mission

As I mentioned in the previous chapter, one of my seminary colleagues opened doors for white Episcopalians and for me by starting the Episcopal Society for Cultural and Racial Unity (ESCRU). That man was John Morris.

A second of those seminary colleagues opened doors to new understandings of world mission by becoming the founder of the Overseas Mission Society (OMS). He was Ted Eastman.[1]

I became part of Ted's organization, and OMS helped a lot of us want to rethink the way mission was conceived and done overseas. That mission was a staple of church life for us in The Episcopal Church, but the thinking that drove it had become stuck. The common understanding among church people was that they would provide the resources to transplant our own model of church to locations overseas, often staffed by clergy from and funded by the home church.

There already were extraordinary pioneers of mission with a far different vision, such as the Anglican Stephen Neill, but the dominant, commonly understood approach was paternal, verging on the colonial. What we learned in Sunday school and carried into our adult pews was often just that oversimplified, as illustrated in *New Yorker* cartoons, with "missionaries" stewing in pots among "villages" of "natives."

OMS under Ted Eastman came to articulate a new vision of a truly interdependent movement in which home churches and mission churches were equals and partners, jointly engaging in bringing the gospel across the globe. This vision was what our mission officers were discovering and teaching, but most of us in the pews were much less sophisticated. Ted and the Overseas Mission Society made great inroads in popular understanding, but change did not happen easily or quickly.

A strategically important program that brought the new concepts into play was the idea of companion dioceses, which established partnerships in mission between a domestic diocese and a foreign one. A major focus was to bring about a new kind of relationship—a companionship rather than a giver-receiver relationship. The national missionary structures of the church worked with the OMS as formal relationships were worked out between dioceses that were domestic and those that were overseas.

In North Carolina, where we were, the Episcopal Diocese of North Carolina entered a companion diocese relationship with the Missionary District of Panama, and a diocesan committee oversaw the relationship. After several years, the term of the relationship—three years—was coming to an end, and our bishop asked me to lead the diocesan committee that would renew the relationship through the national missions office.

I was frankly at a loss. Although I was energized with the ideas the Overseas Mission Society had given us, I was really pretty uninformed with what actually went on in a companion diocese, and I was perplexed about whether or not another term was a good idea.

I happened to know a professor in the sociology department of the University who had the reputation of having helped action programs of various kinds around North Carolina. I approached him to see if he could help us evaluate what we had done during the first term of the companionship. His initial question stumped me. "What were you trying to do?" he asked. "I have to know that if you want to do an evaluation." As far as I know, nobody had ever asked that question. I certainly had no clue.

Fortunately that became the beginning of a period of learning and clarification rather than an end. Gerry Lenski, the professor, worked with me and my committee (now grandly entitled the diocesan Department of Overseas Mission) as we developed a research project that was led by two of Lenski's doctoral students, Donald Stauffer and Wade Clark Roof.[2] It turned out that we had a problem we didn't understand; they needed to come up with dissertations for their doctoral degrees. Our needs turned out to fit.

As a local pastor and volunteer department chair for the diocese, I became a sort of project manager for the research, negotiating relationships and funding with the missions office of the national Episcopal Church. The research efforts taught me a lot about what it took to do careful research that would lead to changed behavior. We also learned how important it was to ask simple questions like "What are we trying to do" before organizing and planning projects. That lesson learned about North Carolina and Panama was essential to us, but it also directly influenced subsequent companionships that were entered by others across the country. Few companionships are entered into any more without first answering the question Gerry Lenski asked me: "What are you trying to do?"

A secondary outcome was that I found myself working with those in the national office of the church and learning how to negotiate program ideas and funding, as well as how to negotiate with multiple entities at the same time. (In truth, it wasn't much different from negotiating with police, businesspeople, and protestors, except the people weren't usually as angry!)

The mission projects we initiated during the next several years in North Carolina and Panama saw us working out the idea of being companions. And we tried to learn from whatever we tried, whether it worked or didn't. We sent several mission trips of young people to assist in camp and conference programs in Panama. Two-dozen lay leaders accompanied the bishop on a tour of Panama. Tremendous growth came for the young people who went to Panama. One of those students, several decades later, when she was working as a public broadcasting producer who developed a national television program about the Washington National Cathedral, told me that she got interested in communication systems when "you sent me to Panama that time." There were many learnings about how racial matters affected people in Panama and in North Carolina. We had to reflect on how racial issues were sometimes different from how they appeared in North Carolina, and sometimes were the same. The experience helped us in North Carolina work on the dynamics of how to desegregate our diocesan camp and conference programs. The Panamanians sent a group of young people because we had sent a group to their camp. We had to deal with the fact that their delegation was a mixed-race group and our camp was still segregated. Both groups did some learning around that!

National interest in companionship and mission, nurtured by the Overseas Mission Society, continued to grow. The House of Bishops developed a major paper on that theme, and distributed a pastoral letter largely written by Stephen Bayne, national leader of the church's mission overseas. The paper, entitled "Mutual Responsibility and Interdependence in the Body of Christ," or, more simply, "MRI" described partnership as the heart of what mission was supposed to be about.

A frustration of mine was in how to help local congregations—which remained my major interest—engage with ideas of mission. So I arranged for our diocesan department to invite Bishop Bayne to the diocese for a series of regional meetings about "The Mission of the Local Church." We engaged vestries and clergy in conversations about how we in local churches could ourselves discover and engage in mission partnerships at home and with Panamanian congregations—or just engage in local mission in our communities. We held seven convocations for clergy and vestries around the diocese. We touched most of the congregations in the diocese, but at the end of it all, instead of generating energy for the local church's sense of its own mission, I was told how great these "conferences on overseas mission" had been. Apparently people's minds were fixed on traditional thinking about mission and could not be redirected as simply as I had hoped. I guess I was learning more than I wanted to know about how difficult it would be to "switch their thinking channel." The convocations were a great experience for me in getting to know Steve Bayne as he and I spent much of a long week crisscrossing North Carolina in my wife's Volkswagen Beetle.

I found a similar difficulty dealing with the concepts of "giving" and "receiving." Our North Carolina congregations did not know how to deal with the idea of receiving in missions. All they had learned was in terms of giving to missions. They drew blanks when asked to conceive of what they would like to *receive* from mission congregations. I gave up on trying—we decided to do what we knew how to do, so we raised money—and the Diocese of North Carolina raised the funds for an Episcopal students' residence at the University of Panama. It connected as "mission giving" at least, because the North Carolina diocese was rightfully proud of its strong history of supporting special ministries.[3] And, to tell the truth, we enjoyed doing something we knew how to do—raise money for mission!

From Planning to Eschatology

By this time my experience—with Industrial Missions across the country,[4] my readings about congregational life and my personal reading, and my efforts to develop the life of the congregation I was serving and to understand the community I lived in—focused me more and more on the technology of planning as the most useful approach to helping change happen. I *was* aware that planning was a terribly rational tool and that life was not all rational. But the systematic steps of a good planning process gave the most promise to being able to help a congregation identify a local task of mission and begin doing it. I was aware that I had been disappointed in the limitations (as I saw it) of city and regional planning to address what I thought of as the human dimensions of community life, but I frankly had not found anything better. Planning seemed to have promise.

One morning that spring, as I sat in my office, I got a phone call—a retired minister in the parish, the Rev. Ed Moseley, asked me if I could get free to go with him to Duke University—it seemed that one of the seemingly interminable list of new German theologians[5] was giving a lecture, and Ed was planning to go. I decided to go with him, not even knowing who the speaker was.

It was Jürgen Moltmann, someone I'd never heard of, who had written a new book, *The Theology of Hope.*

Sitting in that lecture hall was an extraordinary experience for me. Moltmann led me into dimensions of the Scripture I had never plumbed. The lecture took off from the work of Ernst Bloch, a German philosopher heavily shaped by Marxist thinking, but centered on the biblical theme of the Exodus—of the people of God moving out from Egypt toward the wilderness and the Promised Land. Moltmann identified my "itch" for the future not with a technological tool—planning—but with the story of God's people, the story of God's call to his people to leave Egypt for the Promised Land. Things clicked together in my experience and in my mind, and I found myself almost drunk with excitement. I saw new connections between Scripture and my fascination with planning. I began to see how planning was a secular image, perhaps a tool for what in Scripture we called eschatology. "Reaching out toward God's future." It was poetry, while my fascination with planning was prose. It was a prophetic message about God and man, not a technology for maximizing assets. This was authentic *theology,* not just the inchoate musings of a middle-aged philosopher. This was the real thing and what I was looking for in intellectual encounter.

Wow. My head spun as I left the lecture hall (and my head rarely spins after lectures—I'm just not that kind of guy).

Ed and I walked over to my car, and I sensed something was out of kilter. I wondered if the lecture was really turning my mind around. The sky was bright, although it was dark and the sun was long gone. There was a glow all around us. I wondered about Northern Lights— I had never seen them, but I had heard about them—was it that? Or was it my euphoria from listening to Moltmann?

As I cranked up the car, I turned the radio on—perhaps there was a weather bulletin or something. It wasn't the Northern Lights. Or a sizeable forest fire. It wasn't anything like that. I wasn't going crazy. Over the radio the message came.

Martin Luther King had been assassinated.

There were no Northern Lights that night. No forest fire. It was not my excited mind that was burning.

Durham was burning. So were cities across the country, but we didn't know it yet.

Martin Luther King. Dead. My God. My God. In a world of so much sorrow, so much tragedy—he had become to me a symbol of hope. And he was dead. I had come to a lecture on a theology of hope—and that evening my closest image of hope, my symbol of hope, had been killed. Was dead. I couldn't ingest it. It didn't seem possible. I didn't know what to do with it. I went home.

My head continued to spin. All through the racial troubles we had worked with, King had become a primary image of hope. A flawed image—we knew that—but he did represent hope in what seemed hopeless.

For me, there was nowhere to go but where I always took things like that. What do you do? For me there was nothing else—you go to church and lay it on the altar there. That's all I knew to do.

The next morning I got up and went to work. I called Tom Thrasher, an Episcopal clergy friend who had worked with King in Montgomery. King had told us at the ministerial association, as he hugged Tom: "Listen you all. It was not easy in Montgomery. It was hard. And I didn't have many people I could trust. But I want you all to know that this man"—he pointed to Tom—"this man was the one white man I knew I could trust!" I asked Tom to come to our church that night for a special service honoring King. And to preach. We had a service. And did Tom preach! The place was full of people. The police had advised us to stay home, not to go outside, and not to have public meetings like church services, but we had to do it. There were tears; there were mixed feelings of all sorts. We took bread and wine. Did it fix it? No. But it helped. At least I came out with some hope.

Ever since that night I have lived with the contradictory realities that flooded over me that night. The powerful truth that God *is* a god of hope. But also that we live in a world in which hope can seem to die. It is not possible, but both things are true. The impossibility, the rational contradiction, has lived in me every day since that night in April when Ed Moseley and I drove home from Durham to Chapel Hill.

In all my life and work since then, I think those two motifs have been present. The reality of hope. The ever-present possibility of death. They are both enormous truths. As a Christian, I know the ultimacy of hope, but also the ever-present reality of death.

Later that spring I went to Washington, where I spent six weeks in study at the College of Preachers. I soaked in all I could of Moltmann and Pannenburg and all the Teutonic theologians I could get my hands on. I wrote a dissertation, "Towards the New Exodus." I visited Resurrection City, where the poor had gathered in Washington. And I thought and I wondered.

For me, I decided, I *did* have to work on the life of congregations. That was the place, God help me, that I was convinced that faith and hope and love took on human form. And that was where I had to work. As my kids told me, "That's where the rubber hits the road."

World Mission, Parish Mission, and Congregational Life Get Connected

The Overseas Mission Society planned its annual meeting that year under an institutional cloud of which I was unaware. Budget problems were threatening its very existence. It was a threat I would live with soon in a personal way.

My interest in mission, world mission, and congregations got connected when I read a new book, Jean Gottmann's *Megalopolis.*[6] The book described how the American scene had changed, noting that the entire region from Boston to Atlanta had grown together and were linked in every way. The separate towns along what had become Interstate highway I-95 really had become inseparable. The major cities of our diocese were linked together by business, a highway, and common issues, and that linkage made for a new reality.

I saw this as a new mission reality that was not unlike what was happening around the world, so I broached with Ted Eastman the possibility of having the OMS dedicate its annual meeting to exploring that new geographic fact and its implications for mission. I guess I was looking at how the changing shape of the world would affect local congregations' mission. The board of OMS caught the challenge and endorsed the idea. They asked me to start working on it.

I did. I rented a motel in Durham. And I set a date for the meeting.

That's when the OMS decided it had to close its operations. The budget had tanked.

What do you do with a rented motel when the meeting you rented it for had to be cancelled?

You scurry around and whip up something different.

By now I had discovered a lot of people who really were concerned about local congregations. There were books describing how "bad" churches were at the local level: self-centered; sometimes boring. Seminary students were standing in line to get jobs in counseling or chaplaincies or teaching or almost *anything* except going into work in parishes. *The Suburban Captivity of the Churches* by Gibson Winter was a church best seller. The "Death of God" was being featured on the cover of *Time* magazine.

And to be truthful, I had commitments from the Diocese of Washington and the Executive Council of The Episcopal Church to put up $1,000 each for the annual meeting of the OMS. So I had a motel and at least $2,000 for a meeting about the mission of congregations.

I proposed (I do not remember who I proposed it to, but people got on board, thinking "Why not?" I guess) that we hijack the meeting and turn it into something entirely different.

That's how we pulled off a "Consultation on Creative Congregations" that November. The basic idea was that with so much bad talk about parishes and parish ministry, we needed to hear something about how at least *some* parishes were doing impressive ministries. We drew up a list of congregations we had heard about—probably forty or so, spread out among the denominations and across the land—predominately "Mainline," since we didn't know many others. We invited their pastors and several lay leaders to come to the aforementioned rented motel (I think it was called the Downtowner, not far from the Durham Bulls ballpark).

It was a mixed bag. Ted Eastman was there, living with some grief over the loss of OMS, Rolf Lynton (my consultant) was there, and so were the leaders of our diocesan Department of Overseas Mission (they had just completed the evaluation of Panama and were fascinated with what "research" could do). Otis Charles was there—a specialist in creative worship and music, later to be an Episcopal bishop. Bill Wendt and Vienna Anderson (then a lay specialist in worship) were there. The congregations were all over the map. A thoughtful participant, Pat Sanders from Mobile, described the meeting as consisting of two groups: One group included congregations that comprised a bunch of off-the-wall, charismatic people somehow linked to a remarkable, flexible pastor. People who didn't much know about what they were doing or how they were doing it—but they had developed energy and were having a large impact on their city and world. The second group of congregations was made up of equally charismatic and influential people, but they were operating out of a consistent set of principles about living with and planning their lives around change. Probably the one common theme was their commitment to music and liturgy. All of them were working with imaginative music and innovative ways of celebrating Holy Communion.

Not a lot came out of the meeting—except the realization that parish life, congregational life, was alive and kicking. Linkages were formed. Ideas swapped.

People talked about congregations and passed the word.

I went back home to Chapel Hill and my parish, where I was in the middle of a great adventure myself—putting together with my organist and a marvelous parish something I'd wanted to do for years—a folk mass.[7] By late November we pulled it off, and it flew.

The Big Desk

At about this time, a group of national Episcopal leaders had begun meeting to try to "renew" parish life, to "fix" whatever was "wrong" with congregations. They were called the presiding bishop's National Advisory Committee on Evangelism (NACE hereafter), a title slightly embarrassing to Episcopalians, who generally avoid anything associated with the word "evangelism."[8]

Why did they meet? Discomfort with a sense of member loss in some cities was developing. Large downtown congregations across the country were experiencing crises as populations moved to suburbs. There was a sense that we really *needed* to build up membership (the work of Donald MacGavran and the "Church Growth Movement" had already begun to influence the churches—especially those on the more "evangelical" side of things). And, among some, there was a real worry that something was not working well at the congregational level of the church in many places.

NACE had begun thinking of doing an "experiment" to start a breakthrough to new and better ways to do "parish." They were looking for somebody who would lead such an effort. They put together ideas they all had about how to do it, and it boiled down to the common wisdom of that time about how to change things: Get the fifty "best" parish clergy from the "best" parishes across the country, take them all to the middle of the country (like St. Louis), give them full-bore, round-the-clock training, motivate the hell out of them with the best preacher (Billy Graham was suggested), the best liturgical leader (Massey Shepherd was suggested), the best group life leader, the best specialist in spirituality and personal piety, the best . . . name it yourself. . . . *Then* turn those clergy loose and watch what happens. They were beginning to look for somebody who would put it all together, then turn those fifty and their parishes loose and keep track of what the results were. There was a lot of confidence that it would work. I did not share that confidence, but I did share their intensity that something *had* to be done and that the local parish was where it had to happen.

My name came up. I don't think any others showed up. That didn't surprise me. I didn't know anybody dumb enough to try that, myself included.

When the presiding bishop invited me to consider leading that effort, I was aghast, but in spite of myself, I was tempted. On one hand I was absolutely clear that what they proposed had no chance of accomplishing anything. On the other hand, nobody else was even trying to face what was going on in parishes. I remembered how we had hijacked the Durham meeting, and I wondered if one could hijack a project.

After a couple of sleepless nights, I went to New York to see the presiding bishop to tell him "No!"

The presiding bishop was John Hines. When I went in to see him, I think it was the desk that intimidated me most. It looked like a full acre of polished oak in an impressive top floor office in New York City. The desk was totally covered with stacks of paper. And I was a small-town boy from South Carolina.

Behind the desk was the familiar figure. John Hines was someone I had worked with and corresponded with for some time. I had recruited him to do a big diocesan event at Duke Chapel in Durham a few years earlier. It was one of those things we used to do in churches— a big time gathering in the biggest place we could book with massed choirs and the best preacher we could find. A sort of pep rally to get the troops out and charge them up for the annual pledge campaigns. I think we called this one "A Festival of Family Life." That night he had bombed. The sermon didn't work. But he had gone on to become Top Gun in The Episcopal Church. That was the guy across the massive desk from me.

I was intimidated for all those reasons. He and I had had several bits of correspondence about this weird idea of a parish experiment. I do not know what happened in that room, but somehow he made me change my mind, and I left shortly after I found myself saying, "I'll do it!"

***

Excursus: How Did I Get in Front of That Desk?[9]

The road I traveled before standing in front of John Hines's desk felt circuitous. Looking back on it, it seems straight as an arrow. Let me tell you how I got there.

The incidents on the road to that intimidating desk began in the ordinary incidents of a South Carolina boy's growing through childhood in the protected, racist, sexist world of a white middle-class family in a culture so deeply infused with multiple biases that most of us weren't aware of our biases. We were innocently complicit in a society bent out of shape, while not knowing that we and our society were bent. Theologians have language for some of this—they talk of "invincible ignorance" and "original sin." That was us.

It was just how it was. That boy I was made my way through the public schools and social world, privileged but not realizing I was privileged. White, knowing I was not black, glad I wasn't, but not really understanding what the difference was. Rich, for that world, but not knowing that I was rich or what poverty really was. Male, living with rigid stereotypes of masculinity, but at the same time coming of age with an internal battle of hormones and a mix of fascination and fear of the feminine—of *girls*! A good athlete and scholar in the public schools, I was aware that most were less talented at these things than I was, and not at all clear about what to do about those differences. In many ways, then—clueless.

As for church, I was Episcopalian because my mother was. It was a cultural ethos I picked up rather than a theological bias. I realized that most people were not Episcopalians, living as I did in a sea of southern Biblicism, mostly Methodist and Baptist. It may sound funny, but I honestly thought that someday everybody would be Episcopalian.

Three things helped me find my way, and actually pushed me toward John Hines's desk: people, books, and the language of faith.

The language of faith, for me, was indivisible from the patterns of the collects and prayers of the Book of Common Prayer. I learned those patterns first in the Sunday school run by Miss Marie (Gregory) upstairs in the parish house at St. John's parish in Florence, South Carolina. That language occurred only when you were on your knees, in the early days with your elbows on the seat of the chair as you knelt on the bare floor. Backwards.

When sufficiently aged I moved over to Big Church (this was decades before "family services"—Big Church was Adult Church. No mewling infants over there!). You knew Big Church for the "thumps" as the kneelers came down rhythmically during the service: "The Lord be with you." "And with your spirit." "Let us pray!" Thump, thump, thump. And the language that shaped us every week: penitent and obedient hearts . . . erred and strayed like lost sheep . . . O be joyful in the Lord all ye lands . . . O come let us sing unto the Lord . . . do give thee most humble and hearty thanks . . . thine inestimable love . . . be unfeignedly thankful. . . . Those words carved ruts in my soul, rang like familiar bells inside me then, and still do, more than half a century later.

The language worked for me because it gave me ways to express what I knew to be true in so many ways as I grew up. I already knew that I had done what I ought not to have done and I knew I had left undone the things I ought to have done. This language helped me know myself and it placed me in relationship to my God before I knew who I was or who God was. The language nurtured me and gave me space to articulate what happened to me, shaking me to my boots through the emotional jungles of childhood and youth. It gave me a link to reality outside my inner chaos, a link that made even that chaos livable. It was even fun—I remember the silly fun of trying to diagram that language in my English class—unlocking the language of the General Confession in a wild chart of words and phrases. Words became pictures and shapes that sang.

It was more than pure language. It was language's strange ability to open up dimensions beyond itself. Language's function to carry liturgy had come to make sense to me. The words knew me. The words in the Eucharist carried meanings that preexisted, somehow. I knew them to be true to the Word.

And the stories! I *knew* Joseph and Benjamin. The coat of many colors. Joseph was the church sexton and Benjamin must have been my uncle Ben—he was the youngest son in my mother's large family. Not twelve of them, only eight. Abraham was like one of the old men in the parish—sort of an elder. Like a great, great uncle not unlike Uncle Bob who was in the Merchant Marine and showed up drunk on weekends from time to time. David and Paul were real people. They didn't live in other centuries—they were our characters, like General Lee and President Washington. I knew the creation story and it didn't bother me that it couldn't have happened in seven days. Who cares about such details? I knew the story of Paul's ship wreck. Shoot— I had a couple of friends who capsized their boat in the Pee Dee River! Seemed somehow similar.

Hearing those stories was better in the dim light of the parish church—its dark wood of the pews and walls matched the stain of the ceiling. It was a comforting darkness. On sunny days color poured in through the windows and shone on all the brass. I knew it was brass, because my mother helped polish it some Saturdays when she dusted the wooden eagle whose wings held the heavy Bible with different colored ribbons.

The whole thing was sort of one piece. It fit. It was all part of me.

All that pushed me to be in front of John Hines's desk. But people, too.

I'll name a few of them: Preston, Ola, Lacy, Hank, George, and Bill.

Preston's mother and mine were best friends. They went through pregnancy together, so I guess we were doomed to be friends from the beginning, from the sandbox on. We went to Sunday school together and our fathers played golf with each other. Our friendship was as close at the chinaberries on the tree in his backyard where we built a fantastic tree house. (And chinaberry wars between neighbor children—what sticky fun.) In time Pres and I ended up being godparents to each other's children, and even today that friendship is marked by once-a-month lunches in the Shenandoah Valley, halfway between his house and mine. He and I shared the consciousness of something in our culture that we were both uncomfortable about but had nobody to talk about it with except each other. Somehow or other I ran into Richard Wright's book, *Black Boy*. And Preston had found Albert Schweitzer. We read these things and talked about them when nobody else seemed willing to raise the questions that were in us. We kept the friendship going after he moved away.

Ola was a special case. She was black and a servant in my home. Something of what the Old South called a "mammy" is what she was to me. A strange, gracious relationship that existed in the middle of and yet in spite of the hideous social circumstances of our lives as white and black, wealthy and poor. Ola was surrogate mother at times, caretaker at times, household servant at others, and counselor more often than I like to admit. Wise, caring, forgiving. And there was another, deeper relationship—we loved each other. (Tillich was wrong, I think; love can and does exist sometimes even when there is no justice.) Something in her touched something in me in spite of our warring cultures. I remember one day how she, in a strangely shy manner, asked me if she could read a book on my desk (the same *Black Boy* Preston and I talked about). I have no idea how she overcame the barriers to asking that small question, and she and I never talked about the book. Some barriers were just too big. And I remember the time I was covered with bee stings and she sat beside me and chewed several cigarette butts into a poultice she spread over the stings—it sounds awful, but it worked. Over the years, knowing her made me know and feel the bankruptcy of the racial system we both lived in. But that system also infected me with a bone-deep racism that has crippled me over the years in many ways. I hate that racism in me, but I know it's

there. I stamp it down when it comes up, but it still does. I don't kid
myself about that. It's there.

Lacy was a farm boy. Plantation boy is a better description since
his home looked like something out of *Gone with the Wind*. He was rural
and feigned "po buckra" status; I was citified (I mean Florence had
15,000 people!). He and I went to college together and made a formi-
dable debating team. None of our opponents could handle his farm-
yard illustrations and arguments. He went on to a set of high-steeple
Presbyterian pastorates, and we would meet at ecumenical meetings
over the years. It was during his final illness in Tampa that I discovered
the grace with which hospice helped faithful folk take their leave of life.

I met Hank and George in college. Hank and I wrote the gossip
column in the newspaper George edited. Both went to Episcopal seminaries and both became brilliant educators—not conventional academics, but leaders of experiential education. Hank actually did teach
in a seminary until, after his bride's tragic death, he pretty much lost
it to alcoholism. Even then, while he was still a drunk, he helped me
through one very difficult time, making me grow up when I simply
wanted to hide. When friends where he worked carried out an intervention with him, he went into recovery and made it in the pastorate.
George became a bishop and was one long enough to discover how
difficult, if not impossible, that work was. He died too early, maybe
because he tried too hard.

Bill and I met in seminary. And we just kept on running into
each other. I found him brilliant and helpful, but he knocked people
over with his wildly funny wit—the most famous having been a great
research report made up from thin air about how clergy tenure (and
all the clergy at that time were male) was determined by, well, as he
put it, "the length of the pastor's tenure." You cannot imagine what
he did with that concept. Try. If you get it, you'll die laughing as we
did, but you'll also realize why I didn't quote it. He was one of the
best preachers I ever heard, and he had more plain wisdom than anybody I know. He was an extraordinary consultant when I needed a
consultant; an extraordinary friend when I needed that. And what a
companion. I will always remember several hours with him and his
beloved Lib. She was dying in their handmade Alabama home. Bill,
generally a pretty lousy cook, served pecan waffles to the three of us
on Lib's sick bed. The three of us laughed and talked—she, occasionally going silent as the drugs hit her—for several brilliant hours.

I named two books that pushed me—Wright's *Black Boy* and several of Schweitzer's, including his classic *The Quest of the Historical Jesus*. But growing up included floods of books. Early on, sitting in closets in friends' houses, devouring comic books. Bicycling to the town library during the summers, lugging basketfuls of books home. There must have been a couple of dozen books by Joseph Altsheler about the pioneers and the frontier (years later I discovered the only other Altsheler aficionado I know of—George McGovern). History, biography, anything on paper. Benvenuto Cellini, Henry Adams, Gibbon, Chaucer, Whitman, Bernard Devoto, Douglas Southall Freeman. Junk too. Lots of junk.

So part of who John Hines was meeting was shaped by a lifelong exposure to books, a bunch of deep relationships, a strong if flexible basic faith, a deep engagement with learning. A sense of the mystery deep inside. And a good bit of pigheadedness about the local congregation.

***

I did not want to say "Yes" to him. I'd already told Polly that I was going to New York to tell him, face-to-face, that I couldn't do it. I wanted to stay in Chapel Hill to build what I knew the local church could be with the people who had taught me much of what I'd come to know.

I don't know what he said. I only know I left an hour later having agreed to lead "Project Test Pattern." I was as surprised as anybody. I had little real interest in national church structures, and I had never thought those structures much cared about the local church.

But I think I believed the John Hines really did care about what the local church might become. I put my money on him.

Thank God for Polly. When I got home, she told me two things: First, I had to get clear what I *could* accomplish, and see if the committee would buy *that*. Then she told me she would divorce me if I tried to add that job on to continuing to be the parish pastor in Chapel Hill.

I wrote a paper, "The Parish Is the Issue," in which I tried to outline what I thought could be done, proposing a three-year project. I think I really sold a pig in a poke—what we actually did was not what the paper said—but the board agreed to go ahead with me. We went from there and didn't look back. Maybe it was only fair, since they had given *me* a pig in a poke too: There was money for only five months. I guess we were even. I wanted to hijack the project and they wanted to hijack me!

I said "Yes," and we planned to begin in June 1969.

At the end of May, on Ascension Day, 1969, we celebrated as a parish in the amphitheater of the University of North Carolina with a festive service of the Mass of the Holy Family. Shortly after that, we left for Washington, where I had contracted to rent an office from the Washington National Cathedral. Why Washington? Three reasons: It was *not* New York, where the denomination's offices were. It was a city with three airports, and I would be traveling a lot. Washington also had extraordinary resources and ideas about church development and clergy development. These included James Anderson, Jack Harris, and Jean Haldane on the staff of the Diocese of Washington, specialists in education, organization development, and clergy training; John Fletcher and Bennett Sims, specialists in theological education and continuing education for clergy; Tilden Edwards of the Metropolitan Ecumenical Training Institute; and John Denham's Mid-Atlantic Training Committee. I have always liked to be surrounded by creative people.

PART 2

THE PARISH IS
THE ISSUE

CHAPTER 6

Project Test Pattern

Working through the First Model

There were about thirty of us who met at Virginia Theological Seminary for the first effort to kick off what had been named Project Test Pattern. It was June 1969.

The project was named by Bob Brown, then bishop of Arkansas, who had been selected to lead the presiding bishop's National Advisory Committee on Evangelism. Brown chose the name for the pattern television stations used each morning before airing their regular programming. The name Project Test Pattern was intended to indicate the temporary and experimental character of the project itself. It was also prophetic in that three years later, having completed its experimental life, the project self-destructed.

At the seminary that day, six congregations were represented by the rector and two or three lay leaders. They were responding to a pretty vague invitation to engage in a project for strengthening their parish ministry. The invitation was vague because the whole thing was a figment of a number of imaginations, combined with a passionate desire to find answers to a decline of congregational vitality felt in The Episcopal Church. The parishes were from East–Simsbury, Connecticut; Bennington, Vermont; Gramercy Park, New York; Jamaica, Long Island, New York; Lynchburg, Virginia; and Whitemarsh, Pennsylvania.

Why these? They were selected in the middle of chaos. People all around the edges of the incipient project suggested people they knew and places they knew about, with a general feeling that, while not on a list of the fifty "best" clergy and parishes that had been dreamed of, they were yet places that were healthy and, in some cases, unusually gifted in lay or clergy leadership. We had culled the original fifty as too many to manage, and accepted the idea of twenty-four, but clustered as four groups of six so as to be more manageable. We did phone calls, we twisted a few arms, we made payoffs for old favors, and we came down to these six for the first conference. By the same method, we were starting to connect with six more for the next gathering on the West Coast.

One thing was clear to me right away. If the presiding bishop invited them and if the presiding bishop paid for it—people were ready to come. Even if we weren't terribly clear about what we were going to ask them to do. That qualifies as one of our first learnings from Project Test Pattern about how parishes—and the church—operate. Not "build it and they will come" as the movie tells it, but "if you pay them and the presiding bishop invites them, they will come!"

Everything was in flux. My family and I had not moved to Washington yet.[1] Decisions about where to meet and who was on the staff of the conference were made on the run. We had no project office. We had a lot of good intentions but only ephemeral plans. As project director, I knew almost nothing about any of the parishes. I was acquainted with two or three of the clergy and none of the laity. I was beginning to know some of the staff persons we had drafted for the conference: Carman Hunter and Al Rollins of the national church staff; Otis Charles, who I understood to be a specialist in "spiritual development," although I was only vaguely aware of what people meant by that; Jim Anderson and Jack Harris from the Diocese of Washington; and Bennett Sims, who was beginning to invent a Continuing Education Program at Virginia Seminary.

The conference happened in early June in Alexandria, and we sent six teams home with plans and skills to "make renewal efforts" in their home parishes. I'm not sure any of us had clear ideas of what was going to happen. One thing I was clear about: Although I was supposed to "watch and record" the hoped-for changes, I didn't have the foggiest idea about the actual situation at any of the six congregations at the moment that their team was deployed. So I began to wonder how I would know what—if anything—changed.

That summer continued in chaos. My family and I moved to Washington at the end of June, we settled in a house, and Project Test

Pattern became a location when I glued a plastic sign to a door in Hearst Hall on the grounds of the cathedral. We finally had a phone number and a mailing address. We shared space for a few months with the Overseas Mission Society, which was closing down its operations. I bought their furniture and sat in Ted Eastman's desk chair for the next twenty years.

Every day I was learning that my earlier misgivings were right—we had no system for finding out what was going on in the six congregations we'd started with, even though the schedule we had started called for us to begin contacting six more congregations on the West Coast. Telephone calls and letters simply did not give us any sense of a baseline of where the congregations were.

I began acting on what we had already learned. As we made contact with potential new congregations—these turned out to be in Tucson, Arizona; Salt Lake City, Utah; Chehalis, Washington; Twin Falls, Idaho; Watts, Los Angeles, California; and Seattle, Washington— I made travel plans to visit each of the congregations for the conference we'd been planning to hold in Berkeley, California, that fall. My plan was to connect personally with them before the conference, at least visit them, hoping to correct for what we had not done with the first group of parishes.

Those visits were eye-opening. The parishes were all over the map. On the whole, the parish leaders were dedicated, able people, but visions about what their parishes were called to be were thin and contradictory. Each of the congregations was unique and so were the communities in which they were located. The clergy were able people— some actually gifted leaders—but their skills went all the way from zero to genius, depending on what you were looking for. Sitting in on things like vestry meetings, I realized that although we had a gifted bunch of people, often their very sincerity and dedication masked a very low capability to plan or organize. I was surprised as I sat in on vestry meetings how little the clergy seemed aware of basic skills of group leadership, like how to run a meeting. I remember going home with one of the rectors after a long, contentious vestry meeting. He said, "My God, I'm glad that's over! I need a drink!" I agreed with him. I discovered that some of the clergy had never been to a vestry meeting before they became a rector.

I knew my instinct had been right. The original dream of a fifty-congregation renewal effort was a pipe dream. Even as I worked to plan the Berkeley conference with the six new congregations, I tried to find trained consultants we could deploy into the congregations we wanted to work with. I began to realize we had to change models from conference-based learning to in-place learning that happened where the congregation actually was. Instead of sending a few leaders to get trained and then bring their learning back, we needed a really new model of "whole parish learning," bringing knowledge to the parish through consultants who came in.

I began visiting with and learning from experienced consultants—George Reynolds (later to be bishop of Tennessee), Jack Wyatt (already bishop of Spokane), Jim Anderson and Jack Harris of Washington, Ray Averett of Baltimore, and my own consultant, Rolf Lynton of Chapel Hill. On their advice I went to a training event for consultants run by the National Training Laboratories in Holderness, New Hampshire. Later I studied with Irv Pollitt and Billie Alban near Boston.

I found other skilled people who would become part of our network, including Ken Allen of Los Angeles and Lynn Young of Seattle. I met Speed Leas of the United Church of Christ, then starting his work on conflict management around Los Angeles. Trevor Hoy, who led the Berkeley Center for Human Interaction, joined our thinking and became host of the West Coast conference.

***

Excursus No. 2: Some Historical Context

I have been talking here about things that happened during the late 1960s. I was born in 1930. A whole lot had gone on since then that influenced the world and the church I was living in. I do not know all of it, but what I knew affected both me and the churches to which I belonged and with which I worked.

The immediate context was a world that had not long ago finished a terrible war. The macro truths I did not experience—the armies and navies in battle. I saw a little of the impact of that far-off reality. Families lost sons. An uncle was wounded in the Battle of the Bulge. I planted and cared for a victory garden and learned to can tomatoes. I bought war bonds and collected scrap iron.

By the late 1940s everything changed. There were new cars. Money. Jobs. Euphoria. Optimism. Rationing ended and everything was going to go back to "normal," everyone said. And normal was expansive. Everything grew. There was a shadow—the Cold War was beginning—but we mostly dealt with it by denial.

That was true in spades for churches. Everyone we knew went to church. Different churches, yes; but church. There were denominational differences, but we weren't on, very much, to why that was. Presbyterians had a strange doctrine we teased them about—something they called "predestination." We who went to other churches didn't know what it meant, and the Presbyterians we knew didn't know either, but we knew how to make them defensive about it. Baptists mostly didn't dance or drink. The joke was that they couldn't have intercourse standing up because people would think they were dancing. Many of the men we knew hid a bottle in their car's glove compartment because their wives wouldn't permit hard liquor in the house, and they would invite visiting men out for a quickie before dinner. Methodists not only wouldn't drink, they wouldn't smoke. In public. And lots of "hard shell" people wouldn't read the funny papers on Sunday or play cards. We didn't know anything about the Catholics, but there was a lot of suspicion of them. We didn't talk much about the Lutherans because apparently a lot of them came from Germany. The differences were mostly things that had been passed down to church members as vague memories, but often the people we knew didn't much know where those memories came from or what they meant.

Public church in those days was mostly Mainline church, as we call it today. The other churches weren't as socially acceptable, and nobody talked much about them. There were quiet, invisible class differences that nobody talked about, but everybody knew were there. Cotillions and golf clubs collected Episcopalians, Presbyterians, the "better class" of Methodists, and a few Baptists. ("Better class" was never defined, but everybody knew what it meant—and could name the people.) Black people did not get on any of those lists, and few people knew their names.

People flooded into all those churches after the war. New congregations were set up and many flourished. Downtown churches moved to the edges of towns before we even learned to call them suburbs. (Ezra Earl Jones wrote *What's Ahead for Old First Church* about some of them.) There they built bigger church buildings.

That flooding in was a major event for the churches. When I came out of seminary in 1955, it was as if the people were riding an incoming tide. This flood was an outward sign of something we didn't know about or have a name for—the Baby Boom we've named earlier—children born to the young families, many of veterans, who set up housekeeping in the 1950s.

Something else came with that flood of people. Money. Parishes that had scrimped and saved to make budget for years through the Depression and the war started repairing and repainting education buildings and building new ones. Assistant pastors and education directors were added to church staffs. The new wealth spread to regional structures. A bishop or area executive became head of a staff, and we built headquarters buildings. Those staffs helped local churches expand their educational and missional programming. Across the denominations a whole new level of infrastructure was built.

I don't think we realized that the new flood of people and money was temporary. We didn't think that it might come to an end after the hothouse time of postwar euphoria wore off. Even less did we realize that the increased staffs of local congregations, judicatories, and national offices were being paid for by a windfall of unusual income.

In our worst nightmares, none of us thought the growth would end or that the budgets that went up every year would hit their peak, then begin to slide downward.

We never thought that with our expanding budgets we were building a religious infrastructure that would begin to choke us to death within twenty or thirty years. We never would have believed it.

***

The Struggle to Reinvent Project Test Pattern

My early doubts about the experimental model we had received at our founding kept getting stronger and stronger. By the end of 1969, with our first conference nearly six months gone and our second just finished, I found I was getting no information from the parishes of the first conference, and in spite of my having visited all of the parishes in the second conference, I had scant insight into what was happening in those parishes.[2] The model of one researcher managing fifty research locations was ludicrous. It was not happening. Insights into parish dynamics were few. We weren't getting anywhere.

Meanwhile what I was learning about a consulting model of change and research was paying off. Summer training with NTL in New Hampshire put me in touch with people leading efforts to develop more effective educational, business, and governmental working groups, and gave me experience using similar skills. I located people across The Episcopal Church who were experts in this same field and got advice from them. Many who had worked in the national education office, especially the Leadership Training Division, were beginning to use consulting skills and knew others in the church who could join our effort.

Sometime that fall it became clear that we had to let go of the experimental model with which we had started and switch to another model—one in which we inserted consultants in the parish, using them as on-site observers of what was happening. I rewrote "The Parish Is the Issue" to convey the new model and took it to NACE, where it was accepted.

By early 1970, the die was cast. We began getting out of the "invitational conference" model of parish renewal based on generating an elite leadership cadre of parishes that could be motivated toward change, parishes the presiding bishop had chosen to lead the church. That was over.

Now we believed change would come from congregations who helped to define where they wanted to go and got help organizing how to do it. It needed to be motivated by the people in the congregation, not by a bishop (even a presiding bishop) or a rector, or even two or three leading vestry members. We didn't articulate it as such, but we were moving from "leadership development for mission" to "organizational development for mission." We *had* put our money on developing a leadership cadre of a few leaders and a rector who would lead from the top. Now we were beginning to look at developing a parish community, leading as a whole, not just from the top.

CHAPTER 7

Congregational Life in Technicolor

Project Test Patter was only a half-year old, but the first model had simply not worked. The original plan did not produce verifiable impact in the experimental parishes, but a new, more consultative model was looking so much more promising. We had, however, learned some things that gave us what we knew would be a better chance.

We would no longer make the decision about the place for experimentation; instead, we would push that decision to the people involved. We asked key bishops to nominate several parishes in their diocese they thought might be willing to try a consultative approach to strengthening parish ministry. The actual decision to participate, however, would only be made after the congregation had an exploratory meeting with a pair of trained consultants. Every congregation could buy in or buy out after they met the consultants and heard what the consultation would entail. And the consultant teams could decide for or against taking them on as client.

This meant that the congregation had to make the decision. And that decision included paying a negotiated fee to the consultant team. I agreed to continue to pay travel expenses out of project funds. But now, a congregation would get in only by making a commitment to the consultant's definition of what was possible and agreeing to foot some of the bill.

If the plan worked, the decision of the vestry to enter the relationship said to us that they were trying to be—in Lewin's language—"unfrozen." They were choosing to try to change. And they had agreed with the consultants on what the consultants understood the change to involve.

We also made some further commitments: The congregation would make the final decision about participating and would pay the agreed fees, and the consultants would not be lone rangers, but would work in pairs.

That was the plan. What we had to do was *find* the consultants who would do the job, get their agreement to this process, and see if they could do the job. Perhaps more important was whether we could turn this project into a learning community tied together with contracts and a contract-writing process. I rounded up consultants any way I could. Phone calls, checking with people who used consultants, locating people who had been through training programs. As we did so, we also added another dimension. Instead of choosing pairs of consultants myself, I chose individuals whose skills as consultants I really knew and asked them to choose and recruit their own teammate. We came to realize that we wanted teams who would trust each other and learn from each other. I couldn't make the teams—the consultants themselves had to make the teams.

As the teams were forming, I started recruiting a training staff and organizing a conference to develop the in-parish work the consultants would do. We arranged to meet at the continuing education center at Chicago University in February 1970.

I think we all went to Chicago with our fingers crossed. The very small public relations bone in me had generated a lapel button—"THE CHICAGO 28,"[1] bright yellow with garish red print—that we used as our insignia. These went along with the cultural buttons that abounded then: "Free Bobby Seale," "The Chicago Seven," etc.

My associate Jim Anderson took leadership of our training staff, and he and I were joined by Carman Hunter, Robert MacFarlane,[2] George Reynolds, Al Rollins, and Bishop Jack Wyatt. Taylor Scott, a doctoral student at Duke University, provided additional observation and input.

We worked at Chicago. We made contracts with each other and with the project. We gave demonstrations and taught each other what we knew—how to assess the life of a congregation; methods of data gathering; community assessment methods; varieties of conflicts and conflict management; how to build vestries into leadership teams; how to test for readiness to change.

We found that these individuals had stores of theory, remarkable working models that groups could learn, and we shared what we knew. By the time the conference was over, we had produced what we called the *Parish Intervention Handbook*, with dozens of designs for particular situations and different groups. And we had tested most of them with each other.

For four days in Chicago, thirty-two consultants and the training staff shared designs they had developed in working with congregations in other contexts. We found that these individuals had stores of theory, remarkable working models that groups could learn. Theories and methods were tested in small groups and as a whole. As time moved, the theories and methods became short essays and design outlines. Before the time was out, we collected a whole book of aids, practical guides, and instructions for designs and duplicated them for the group—our first mimeographed production. As the week of learning ended, each consultant was given a copy of "The Parish Intervention Handbook" to use with client parishes. When we left Chicago, we each had a copy of the handbook, and we had agreed to continue to share designs we developed in our consultations.

Each was also given several optional outlines for consultant reports, which they were to submit after every intervention in a congregation. I promised to circulate reports or information the others submitted as further aids and support for their work.[3]

The time at Chicago was intense, but electric with learning and excitement about the possibilities.[4]

The consultants left Chicago to initiate their interventions with potential parishes. All of them already had day jobs, so we knew it would take them some time to arrange times and places for their visits.

By the end of February, twelve teams of paired consultants headed out with a list of prospects from a diocese near them. One team—which had come in at the end—was an ecumenical team of four to deal with a cluster of congregations in the Washington, DC, area.

The parish consultation phase of Project Test Pattern rested on their shoulders. Would comprehensible information come in? Would the consultants make contracts with the congregations? Would we be able to understand what they were encountering and whether or not their designs were working? Would they actually make a difference in those congregations?

Would it work to have congregations make decisions instead of a far-off executive or bishop? Would it strengthen data-gathering to have a pair of consultants intervening each month rather than a project manager who phoned when he could and visited maybe once a year? We had no guarantees, but that's where we put our money.

An equal question for me—could I hold this together, deal with the disparate consultation teams in different parts of the country, in different dioceses, with their different levels of skill? Could it work?

For some time—silence. Everyone was busy. Consultants had jobs and assignments elsewhere. Parishes had parish activities to push ahead with. Appointments had to be arranged and clarified. Team schedules and parish schedules had to be coordinated. Everything took more time than we wanted it to. Several potential contacts evaporated, or blew up in miscalculations. In spite of our efforts to provide as much clarity as possible, several people got involved without understanding what was happening. Some parishes went to meet consultants expecting magicians with all the answers and were upset to find out that they had to help and do the heavy lifting themselves. Some got excited, but felt the time was wrong.[5]

I got in trouble when the consultants working in Arkansas—the diocese whose bishop was my chairman—communicated what they were to do to the parish in ways that varied a lot from what the bishop, my board chairman, expected. He had not changed *his* dream, but the plan NACE had voted to accept was considerably different. I had a quick unexpected trip to Little Rock to unpack that one.

Nothing dramatic happened. I began receiving consultant reports of data-gathering in congregations, of negotiations and explorations. Some of the reports included insights from directly observed vestry meetings—something I don't think anyone had ever seen before. Each team tracked its own path. Finally one parish consultation contract is signed. And another. Pause. Another. Then "contract rejected." From another pair—silence. From the ecumenical quartet—chaos. Several congregations saw everything differently. We had to redesign. We kept having to redesign. We were hearing what actually was going on, and what was happening was not fixed ahead of time. People reacted to what was going on, and they did not always react the way we expected them to react.

Each case was unique. We should have known it would be that way, but the "common wisdom" took it for granted that parishes were all alike, basically. Well, they weren't. Each had its own slant. Its own agenda. Its own unique, and sometimes strange, decision-making system. They couldn't be pushed to make my schedule. And they did not do what we wanted them to do—they did what felt right to them.

I went through the spring and summer picking up bits and pieces in the consultant reports. One consultant pair worked hard, but couldn't seem to get around to writing anything up—and my system depended on written reports! I called Rolf: "What can I do?" I asked him. "Buy them a couple of tape recorders," he said. I did. (Then I had another problem—I had to find somebody who could type up a report on a cassette tape!) But it worked. I talked to the consultants directly a lot too.

My office was filling up with reports. Exciting reports telling things I don't think anybody had seen before. But nobody was looking at them but me. I began realizing that I would need help organizing material from the different consultations, and I started looking around for somebody who could help. I found a seminary student at Virginia Seminary who wanted to do some church research. Elisa DesPortes went to work even though we had no money to support her work. I sent SOS messages to the presiding bishop's office, receiving assurances of support but no money. (Minor learning: People in administrative offices often are not aware of the operational necessities of the people charged with doing the work!) Finally some money came.

I decided to pull together a regional group of the consultants for a face-to-face meeting in Birmingham, Alabama. I felt I needed to know what was really happening in these consulting relationships, and I thought retrieving their experience in a face-to-face meeting would educate us all.

I had no idea what would happen. I expected to learn about the consultants and how they worked, planned, and reflected on their work. But the *big* thing was I got to look into how congregations actually worked. It was a level of data I had never seen before, and I doubt anyone else ever had either. I was able to watch—as if having been perched on the wall (my usual reference point) of the boardroom as ordinary parish members argued, talked, joked, fought, collaborated, planned, and speculated about what they were doing or trying to do. How very smart laypeople rolled over on what they knew and deferred to their pastor; how aggressive people took over from more reticent ones; how good ideas got swamped under bickering about something somebody remembers going wrong last year; how some people kept coming up with ideas others didn't even hear. How issues or arguments replicated themselves in meeting after meeting, even after decisions had been made.

Those congregations were a zoo of human communication and miscommunication.

I realized how little I had ever known about what went on in church meetings. The written materials I had heard before tended to be sermons (or sermonic books) written by clergy-types telling what ought to be. Some inspired stuff, but generally not based on knowledge, research, or data.

Having smart consultants, equipped to look, see, and report, I was able, as it were, to look inside what was going on. Metaphorically I began understanding it as if I had been rowing a boat across a river all my life—and suddenly I discovered there was a glass bottom in the boat; I had a chance to look through the glass bottom for the first time and see things that had been there all along but that I'd never seen before.

As I remember, we all began to see what was happening when Harry Pritchett and Martha Adams, the consultants working with a parish in north Alabama started reporting. Harry gave us all a log of what they had seen, done, and observed. The rest of us were drawn into their narrative. Exclaiming about similar or different things they had discovered, noting particular dynamics between different actors, and how the different actors (like "rector," and "warden," and "treasurer") interacted with each other, sometimes imaginatively, sometimes as if by rote. It was obvious to everyone that the role of clergy was somehow more critical in each place, often in different ways. The lay-clergy relationship was some kind of key to what happened. We could look at that in different situations, and each situation came out of a different historical context, related to how the roles had been played in earlier times in the congregation's life. At times we could even see dim outlines of past experiences of the parishes, with different clergy and different lay leaders, and we listened to stories of painful as well as joyous times they had known before.

All of a sudden, congregational life turned into Technicolor. Like when Dorothy got to Oz.

I'd been digging and digging, knowing that it was in the life of the local congregation where, as my kids would tell me, the rubber hits the road. Well, all of a sudden I knew that was true. That's where it all came from. I had hit pay dirt.

CHAPTER 8

Growing Interest in Congregations

My work was pulling me into a number of other enterprises related to the work of clergy and parishes. I was called to speak at the founding meeting of the Academy of Parish Clergy (APC) in Bloomfield Hills, Michigan, and to work with the group beginning to form the Society for the Advancement of Continuing Education for Ministry (SACEM), as well as with the Association for Creative Change (ACC). All of these organizations were coming into being pretty much at the same time, reflecting a desire among local clergy for collegiality and pro-fessionalization—perhaps a current related to the founding of PTP and its focus on congregations. They were mostly aimed at the effec-tiveness of the clergyperson. James Glasse's book *Profession: Minister*[1] was becoming popular, and the National Council of Churches was studying stress in ministry under Edgar Mills.

The carefully controlled set of consultants we had recruited and trained did not stay carefully controlled. Others with skills and interest in our questions began coming to share what they were learning. Still others were working through us to get access to the strong training program that John Denham's Mid-Atlantic Training Committee had developed for consulting with congregations. Two seminary students came to us to inquire about MATC training, but I dissuaded them—assuming they were too young and inexperienced to take on the con-sultant role. They persisted, I relented, and Bob Gallagher and Alice Mann went on to become stellar consultants. Still another pushed in with a recommendation from Robbie MacFarlane and a desire to test the use of consulting skills as a pastor serving during the period

between permanent or "settled" pastors, as his Presbyterian structures described them.[2]

Meanwhile, I had to see that each consultant report was received,
responded to, and preserved. As consulting reports rolled in to the
office, Robbie MacFarlane began pushing us to publish what we were
learning. I was skeptical, but Elisa DesPortes started pulling together
material so that we could produce what we were beginning to call
"case stories." The very name indicated some of what we had learned.
I had a strong feeling that we could not call them "case studies," which
would have put us in the role of the expert. I wanted to be in the role
of reporter, with the reader working to be more expert in his or her
own system. I wanted the cases to be open so that the people who read
them could discern the meaning in terms of their own work. I did not
want people to see them as guides, but as descriptions of what those
people did in that place, leaving open such questions as: How does
that place differ from yours? How did those people respond to what
they saw? Do you see things they may have overlooked? How does that
tell *us* to discern what we need to do in our different situation?

Without really planning it, we were already beginning to be dis-
tributors of knowledge. The October quarterly report listed as available one case story, several smaller publications about PTP, *The
Parish Intervention Handbook,* and several magazine articles, mostly in
Episcopal publications.

Of more substance, we had also begun encouraging networks
of consultants into training and collaborative work in dioceses with
which we had substantial connections—North Carolina; Central New
York; Newark; Alabama; Olympia; Texas. We were also in conversation with other dioceses that were working parallel tracks, including
Tennessee and Mississippi.

In addition to our work with the Presbyterians and United
Church about "clusters," we had also been called in for consultations
or work with Missouri Synod Lutherans, LCA and ALC Lutherans,
United Methodists, Catholics, and Brethren.

The fact that I was being called on in many places to give addresses
or teach in dioceses, consultations, or congregations even though we were
just beginning to be able to see into congregations reminded me increas-
ingly of the adage, "In the land of the blind, the one-eyed man is king."

Underneath all of this good work, however, was the reality that
Project Test Pattern was only a three-year experiment, and decisions
about its future—and mine—would have to be made soon.

CHAPTER 9

"Responsible Closure"

As we drew toward the planned end of the funding for Project Test Pattern, two realities got clear: (1) PTP *was* ending, not morphing gradually into something else or, the way many things in the church did, simply oozing away and disappearing; and (2) *something* needed to come next. Congregations did need help, and PTP had made it clear that some changes were possible. There were many people who would love to see PTP continued, somehow.

I was more ambivalent than was comfortable. If PTP ended, I would need a job. I had been given a chance to learn a lot, and I felt a real commitment to trying to use what I had learned. Also there was unfinished business about congregations, questions that needed to be answered, learning that needed to be connected with those who could use it.

Closing PTP was not easy for me. Working so hard to keep the thing going, and excited as I was about what we had begun to learn, I found myself enormously conflicted over what we were planning to do. I remember two things from that time—a vivid dream and an intense argument. The dream occurred several times, probably in 1973. The fact that I remember it so vividly tells me how deeply I was experiencing profound uncertainty and anxiety.

The dream repeated itself several times, with different details but the same message. In the dream, I'd wake up in the middle of the night, in a bed beside one of my own children. A menacing, shadowy figure passed me a pillow and told me I had to smother the child I knew to be my own. I remember even today the horror of the experience.

In the dream, I really believed I had no option. I'd usually wake up right then—but the feelings of horror stayed with me. Did I pick up the meaning about killing off my own offspring? You bet your life.

The argument was with the project associates who had become my guides and aides, working right beside me in much of the project. It happened at a "Findings Conference" in January 1973, as the project entered its final year. We gathered sixty people who had been involved in PTP in Mobile, Alabama, to sort out what we had learned from our different perspectives.[1] The argument was over whether to go ahead with the plan we had when we started—to see PTP as a temporary system, an intervention in the life of the church, *not* as a permanent, ongoing organization. I was for going on. The associates, almost to a person, were opposed. It was a hard, emotional, fight, but I lost, hands down. There were bitter words and even some tears—mostly from me. I think I realized they were right.

The next day, as the conference closed, the Eucharist carried a heavy emotional load, and I—as the celebrant—almost couldn't pull it off. It had become clear to us that what we had done had touched a lot of people in the church and had generated a lot of positive interest—and the better politicians in our crowd were convinced that if it came to a vote in The Episcopal Church, we could probably win. But from somewhere, someone coined the phrase "responsible closure," and it carried the day. We began thinking of what that might mean in two dimensions—as a witness to our theological conviction that death was not an end; and secondly, as an expression of a belief that some things do need to die, a fact about which the church seemed to be in denial. We felt that to be a lesson the church needed to know, and that we had learned in our work. We had one year to live into this understanding.

And I needed to figure out how I would make a living.

I had started working on this issue, as part of my work on the project. It had already become clear to me—as director of the project—that my own skills and capacities were important to think about. If we chose to do something as a project that I, personally, had no skills at, was uninterested in, or simply didn't want to do—the project probably would spin its wheels a lot and not accomplish much. So I had contracted with Bart Lloyd, head of the Mid Atlantic Career Development Institute, to take me on. He helped me analyze my strengths and weaknesses, helped me locate better my passions and my aversions. He provided practical management guidance. For example, I've never been very good with money and budget things, so we made sure that we could get people good at those things when we had those issues to deal with.

Later, as we drew nearer the end of the project, the resources Lloyd had brought to me in the beginning provided clues for where I should look for employment, and I sought his advice again. I was getting enough visibility across the church that people started inquiring if I might be available for this or that job opportunity. A couple of nominating committees at theological seminaries began nosing around to see if I might be open to leading a seminary. Several dioceses had committees asking if I might be available to be elected bishop. Both directions were enormously flattering to me, and even exciting in prospect. Fortunately, Lloyd helped me look at the data of what I did well and poorly, what turned me on and turned me off— and it quickly became obvious to me that although both were very exciting, attractive roles to me, I really hated doing what most bishops had to do and what most seminary presidents had to do.

On the possibility of being a bishop, I finally articulated it to myself this way: I'd *love* the trappings of the job, the kinds of liturgical roles possible, the leading of great convocations, the fascinating garb some bishops wore, like purple shirts and those crazy hats. I'd love all that stuff, but every morning I would wake up, hating to go to the office to do what I saw most bishops having to do, day in and day out. My answer, I used to say, to the problem: I should buy purple pajamas!

Whatever I ended up doing, I remained convinced that *something* needed to be done with the work of Project Test Pattern. What had we learned that would give us guidance about what we, or others, needed to do to build on the learnings of Project Test Pattern? What had this project, this way of working with local churches, discovered about what congregations should address?

In the latter half of 1973 I began meeting with others to think about this question. The core group was made up of Jim Anderson of the Diocese of Washington, Tilden Edwards, director of the Mid Atlantic Ecumenical Training Institute, and Jack Harris also of the Episcopal Diocese of Washington. All four of us were white, male, Southern, and Episcopalian—which only shows how far we had yet to move. Within a larger circle were other gifted people, including John Fletcher, then starting Inter/Met Seminary, Herb Donovan, a parish priest from Montclair, New Jersey, Pamela Chinnis, Verna Dozier, and Helen Eisenhart, lay leaders or wardens in Washington parishes, and Ed White, the executive presbyter of the Washington Presbytery.

Those conversations led, by late 1973, to drafts of project proposals and conversations with some funding agencies for an ecumenical entity that would follow the path the Episcopal project had begun. It would work on parish development in all sorts of congregations, not just Episcopal parishes. It would facilitate the use of organizational development consultants in churches. It would help to shape conversations about continuing education of clergy. It would, overall, provide a framework for making strategic interventions in religious institutional life.

CHAPTER 10

In Media Res

It was awkward, starting this new entity, which we came to call the Alban Institute. More than we expected.

Up to this point, I had been a sort of loose Episcopal denominational functionary, carrying out a project sponsored by the presiding bishop of The Episcopal Church. That located us in Project Test Pattern as an actor in a set of relationships. Our "world" was the world of denominations, a network of corporate religious organizations and structures in the United States with connections to entities in other parts of the world. Our "neighborhood" was the Protestant Mainline denominations—that was where we related most often and with whom we had the most conversation.

What I had no way of realizing, but do now, was that the familiar world of denominations was evaporating around us, and that the neighborhood was disintegrating. For a long time we lived on in the never-never land as if they would go on forever: denying the incremental dislocations and disappearances that suddenly appeared in our trusted systems.

Working for the presiding bishop of The Episcopal Church gave us a "place" in never-never land. It seemed secure and strong.

As presiding bishop he carried a pretty impressive title, and at the time I was both impressed and intimidated by him. I've come to realize things weren't what I'd thought they were.

"Presiding bishop" as I experienced it was actually a pretty new piece of The Episcopal Church furniture. Indeed, there wasn't much furniture of any sort in the institution. The denomination itself was something of a mystery—"sort of" related to the Church of England that had "founded" it. But even *that* was "sort of" a mistake. A bunch of people who sailed across the Atlantic to make their fortunes, because they were English, had understood themselves to be Anglicans in faith, and they carried the sense of belonging to the Church of England—a church that was "episcopal" because it had bishops! But when they crossed the Atlantic, they forgot to bring along the bishops, so it was awkward to call it an "episcopal" church. It would take almost two centuries to figure out how to get a bishop across the ocean. Nobody asked them to start a church. Nobody sent them to be a church. But they were English and had grown up in a culture that was churched, so that's what they took with them. Even that early, they took a chaplain along, and they took along the Book of Common Prayer.

When I was young, there were Episcopal churches around—not a lot, but some. They were thin on the ground, obviously; it had been the Church of England, and Americans had fought a war to get the English off their backs. So a Church of *England* was a public relations problem.[1] There was not much of a "center" to the American church, just a bunch of regional clusters called dioceses, each with a bishop—by now they'd figured how to bring them across the ocean. They became national, but fudged even that, choosing "confederation" rather than "federation" as their model of togetherness, leaving secession and nullification part of their DNA to be trotted out every time a controversy loomed. They even had national meetings every three years, whether they needed to or not. All the bishops met together then, and one of them was elected to hold the gavel for their meetings. He was called the "presiding bishop." That was also when the house always sat in order of consecration, leaving the oldest bishops in the front row (which obviously was widely known as "death row"). The presiding bishop was the person who handled the gavel and refereed the Roberts' Rules at those meetings.

During World War II, with institution-building going on all over, from General Motors to the Pentagon, Episcopalians got with it and organized themselves. They divided their work into departments, organized a national staff, and made the presiding bishop head of that staff. They never got an office for it all until 1963. Somewhere along the way they started calling him (and, until 2006, they were all a him) a primate. Presbyterians, Lutherans, and others made similar moves—even the National Council of Churches built a headquarters they nicknamed the "God Box" on Riverside Drive in New York, right next door to the "cathedral" the Rockefellers built for Mainline Protestantism. It was a sign of the times.

Was all this organizational tinkering that different from Alfred P. Sloan knitting together General Motors or J. P. Morgan inventing US Steel and General Electric? It *was* different, but it was also a response to a cultural flow that energized and reshaped America and the world, affecting how people related to each other, worked, and built their society and their homes.[2]

The man the church elected to wield the gavel at bishops' meetings was given the job of running the national headquarters.[3] It really wasn't that long ago. I remember shaking the hand of the man who first functioned as this new presiding bishop, a neat man named Henry Knox Sherrill. That's how recent it all was. How really new.

The man who intimidated me and had become my boss was John Hines, and he was the presiding bishop while I was working on Project Test Pattern from 1969 to 1974. That's boss, "sort of." Actually I worked for the committee that "advised" him—the National Advisory Committee on Evangelism.

No, it probably wasn't particularly clear. The organizational structures were fairly imaginary—but they were understood to be real.

Probably *all* the denominational structures had a similar Peter Pan kind of reality—as long as we believed in them, they worked. As long as you believed in them, they gave you structures and relationships, roles and tasks. By the 1980s and 1990s, most of our belief in these Peter Pans was wearing thin. Joseph Bottum, in *An Anxious Age,*[4] describes how the "whole world" of Mainline Protestantism provided a framework for understanding America's values, politics, and understanding of itself until, in Bottum's phrase, that center "evaporated" in the late twentieth century. The story being told in this book happened during the period Bottom defines as the time when that evaporation was happening. Living inside that change, we did not realize the large displacements that were occurring in our environment.

I did not understand all that then, and am only now—forty years later—beginning to understand what happened. Working for the presiding bishop in those days, I had a location. A set of relationships. People I could call on for help. A financial system that had rules and could make allocations to fund things. An orderly set of processes by which things were decided and done. It was a world we know as denominational religion, that took its shape in the United States from its predominant voice—"Mainline Protestantism." It was, indeed, a whole world; a world that itself was in turmoil.

My advisors in Project Test Pattern had made a decision for "responsible closure" when we concluded our originally contracted three years of work. We did not fully understand what we meant, but it had to do with a particular project within one denomination—The Episcopal Church. The closure I understood to be the end of a particular project sponsored by that denomination. That I understood. But starting this new organization would mean stepping outside the frameworks for working on "religious" issues, outside the framework of denominational systems and structures that had grown up across the country.

In the world I had worked in, I sort of knew how to play the game of denominations and projects and budgets. The world I stepped into did not recognize the rules of that game. Neither did I.

CHAPTER 11

Best Laid Plans

When I went to my office—rented from the National Cathedral in Washington, DC—I stepped into a new world. It was physically the same office as the one I'd worked in for the Episcopal project I led, so it didn't feel very different. I thought I was starting a project like the ones that abounded in the religious world. After another argument, we named it the Alban Institute (after its geography—the cathedral sits on Mount St. Alban—since we couldn't agree on a more functional title).

It was a world that was outside all the structures I had known. Technically I remained an Episcopal clergyman, but I no longer served in an Episcopal job or under an Episcopal bishop. I remained Episcopalian in identity only as a member of a local congregation and as a member of the Episcopal clergy pension system (so long as I voluntarily paid the assessed fees).

I had done due diligence. I knew the formal structures around me were in many kinds of change, and that the particular project I had led, Project Test Pattern, was ending. I did not realize that I had inadvertently already violated the system we all lived in—I had collaborated with, consulted with, served contracts with—not just Episcopalians, or even primarily with Episcopalians, but with anybody in any denomination who was willing to work with me. Now, with some colleagues, I had put together a plan for building a new structure, and we had completed a grant proposal to help it get started. That was to be my future, as leader of a project we hoped would be funded by foundations, and that whole thing had been put in a proposal that awaited funding at its next meeting.

I went to my office the first day, February 1, 1974, proud of what we had done. The day before, we mailed off the manuscripts for books from Project Test Pattern work that would come out later in the year.[1] We had shipped off three sets of project archives. I had wrapped up what I could wrap up: Bill Yon's remarkable paper on clergy transition, "Prime Time for Renewal," was in print; two other projects were done[2] and put to rest.

I had assets. A number of monographs and several books produced by the Episcopal project I had led. I had numerous contacts from my work with leaders of other denominations who had responded to my initiatives. I had a shoebox full of names and addresses on index cards, and I had some credibility with the people on those cards. More than that, I had a store of learnings—some identified in the books and articles we had already produced. And I had considerable confidence that our approach worked in religious institutions—one could identify issues, gather and interpret data, try different methods of inducing change, and distinguish between efforts that led nowhere and efforts that paid off. I knew people didn't change until they decided they wanted to change and were willing to participate in real effort. I knew that outsiders with ideas and processes could help change happen if they could find a way in, and generate a relationship of genuine trust, and I knew that the technology of organization development provided helpful methods. We had learned to train consultants in those methods, and we had stimulated several groups in the churches to train more consultants.

There were liabilities I brought as well. I had only three months of salary for myself and one for my secretary. There would be no further financial support from the sources that had financed the last three plus years. I had warning too: In all those closely organized systems with budgets and commitments, our income had never been secure. I had never experienced more than two month's expenses actually in the bank. But now there was nothing. All our eggs were in one basket, which sat in the office of a national foundation that had given assurance of support. I did not recognize that stepping out of Project Test Pattern was a big deal—that I was crossing a boundary into a new country. What may be even more important, I did not see at all the situation that Bottum's book and my own subsequent learning made clear—that the set of religious institutions and relationships within which I planned to work were themselves evaporating before my eyes.

I set out immediately to build on what I had going for me. Two national groups had offered contracts for me to lead program efforts they were planning, and a seminary had asked me to lead a continuing education program about what the projects had learned about congregational dynamics. The Joint Strategy and Action Committee of the National Council of Churches had asked me to staff a series of conferences around the country, and the American Baptist Personnel Services wanted to adapt our learnings about changing pastors for their regional staff leaders in another series of conferences in different regions of their church. I began making those arrangements while waiting for the foundation grant and planning distribution of Project Test Pattern publications.

I was in Richmond, teaching in a continuing education event at Union Presbyterian Seminary when I received the telephone call from the foundation. The board of the foundation had rejected the advice of the staff that had worked with us, and turned down our grant.

I think I had known in the back of my mind that I had gone pretty far out on a limb, but I also trusted the people advising me, those whose ideas I had pulled together for the proposal, and the signals we had received from the foundation. In fact, that telephone call in Richmond told me that the limb had been cut off. Nothing. Nada.

I had no Plan B.

My response was natural, I think. I panicked. I finished my gig in Richmond in a total fog. I went home with no plan, no idea where to go next. My wife and children jumped in and did all they could think to do. They took me to the movies. We saw *Blazing Saddles,* that wild comedy—and I laughed until I cried. And I really did cry.

That was February 18, 1973. Exactly eighteen days earlier I had crossed the river, gluing an ALBAN INSTITUTE sign to the door to the office. I didn't have money to pay the rent on the office.

Back at the office the next day I did what I could think of. I called the people I'd agreed to do jobs for and revised the terms of what I would do. Instead of doing my work for free, as I'd generously suggested earlier—I had to charge a fee.

I don't think I realized I was repeating what I had done when our first model of Project Test Pattern bombed. I switched from "church work is all done for free" to "do you want to work with me enough to pay for it?'"

From my end, it was the only thing I could do. From their end they had to consider Lewin's question—"Are you willing to try to change? Ready enough to pay in order to change?" I had no idea that's what I was asking. But in fact asking them to pay a fee to work with me was a crossing of the Rubicon. On one side of the river, the presiding bishop, or somebody with authority and money, is asking you to change. On the other side, *you* are making the decision, the commitment, that you want to engage, to work, to change. On one side of the river, you did what your "betters" told you to do, and they paid the cost. On the other side of the imaginary river I was actually asking them to join me—*they* were taking the authority to choose what they wanted to do and agree they were willing to pay to do it. In the long run, I'm convinced I was on the right side of the river.

The change was no easier for me than it was for them. I did not know how to charge for my services, and I did not know how much to charge. I did know then—and I got to know it every day in the Alban Institute—that I was violating the customs of religious groups.[3] Almost nobody either charged a fee for doing a job[4] or even *talked* about what it cost to provide a service.[5] Indeed, it was considered bad form even to bring up the subject of money.

Charging fees did not solve my financial problem, but it clarified my options. I was lucky. Most of those who wanted my services got on board with the new system, not without having to deal with budget issues of their own.

My own budget problems were escalating, with no regular income in sight. Two or three small foundation proposals were still active, but nothing had been secured.

By early March, though, we saw the cliff's edge approaching. When my advisors and I met that month, we had to face facts. Our costs were running about $4,000 a month, and we were already $3,000 in the hole. As we looked ahead, we saw no resources we could count on. Some fees were contracted for, but bills were outrunning what we could expect to come in. We bit the bullet. The Alban Institute was a great dream, but we couldn't pay the rent and phone bill, much less cover salaries for my secretary and for me. So, in our meeting that afternoon, we made a list of what we had to do to close down, and when we had to do it.

The next morning I pulled out the list of what to do and when, and started to work the list. As I started, Wilma Swanson, my secretary, called from the other office. "Loren," she said, "The phone's for you." "Who is it?" I asked, conscious of the phone bill. "It's Mac, calling from Houston." Mac had been one of our consultants, a Roman Catholic layman who worked for NASA. He had agreed to work in Project Test Pattern on a consultant team because he knew organizational development and thought it might be useful in churches, including his own Catholic parishes. I knew and liked him, and had used him in several meetings to demonstrate ways of working with organizations.

Problem? He always called collect. I called back to Wilma, "Is it collect?" I asked. If he was calling collect, I couldn't accept the call, based on a decision we'd made the previous afternoon. "No. He's paying," she replied. "I'll put him on."

He picked up my mood right away. "What's the problem?" he asked. "Well, Mac, we just had to realize that Alban's a great dream, but it just can't happen." "What do you mean?" he asked. "We're out of resources, Mac. We're $3,000 in the hole right now, and that'll be $7,000 by the end of next month. And no resources to fill the gap."

"That's too bad, Loren. I'm sending you a check today for $7,500. Got any other problems?"

That's how close it was. I had no idea Mac *had* $7,500. I had no idea where else to go, but that was the signal we needed. It turned out that Mac found a donor who gave $25,000 more. Two of the small grants came through; one for $5,000, the other for $20,000 a year for two years. With those, plus a lot of scrambling and charging for whatever we did, we got the space to go on.

The reality of our need to generate whatever it cost to run the institute from what we did hit hard in those early months. It shaped much of our life. But during those early months, my advisors and I struggled to clarify where we needed to start and what we needed to keep at the center.

A couple of clear themes stuck with us. First was a deep, primal conviction that the local congregation represented our special call, our reason for being. Let me be clear—if embarrassingly personal—that I, and the "institute," "team," or "group" I wanted to form and lead, were being summoned to do something to help what we called congregations become local embodiments of a caring, ministering community of the people of God. We didn't talk about it always in such clearly faith-based language, but that is what I wanted to be and do.

We came with baggage. Good and bad. The bad was obvious. Congregations, even for many of the people who made them up, had come on hard days. They were trashed by many as wasteful, irrelevant, impotent, and distracting (and there was evidence easily at hand to prove all those charges). Many fine people had given up on them, including many fine clergy who had burned out working for them. Then, too, our culture was in the middle of changing from one in which the stuff of religion was central and religious institutions were simply the given heart of ordinary life to one in which ordinary consciousness was much more skeptical of the religious, and religious institutions were marginal to life.

But we came with good baggage too. Historical stuff, like how this strange local embodiment of faith—the religious congregation— had morphed its way through centuries, passing on a story of faith and a vision that human life was called to wholeness and to the healing of life and the world. I felt that call and story, and I claimed it for myself and for those who became colleagues in our work and life. We were aware of generations of people of genuine faith and knew ourselves to have received much from those who passed that faith on to us. We were short on money and wisdom, but we did have an enormous endowment of faith, experience, and knowledge passed on to us by those generations—even if some of that heritage had developed sclerosis of the arteries.

Having started amidst all the ambiguities of local congregations, I think we refused to believe the bad news and chose to work for the vision. We had learned, in just a few short years, that it was possible to learn about congregations and how they worked. We had found some ways they could be encouraged or even changed toward a larger vision. We had discovered some fulcrums from which to lever movement in recalcitrant organizations, and we had learned from many who worked in the behavioral sciences about how change happens in other settings.

That's why, when our plan A was rejected by the foundation, I knew there was no turning back, even if there was no plan B. So we plunged in—without a plan, but with a vision, with some early hunches and a few things we had learned—and started surviving. Like the bumblebee, which is supposed to be aerodynamically unable to fly, we started flapping our wings.

The immediate questions had to do with an excess of opportunity (there were so many possibilities), the absence of resources (zero chance for regular support of the institute itself), and a turbulent environment of religious effort, need, imagination, and incoherence. Let me begin by describing the world in which this incipient institution was being born.

The Mainline churches, especially in the Washington area, were awash with ideas and programs—all sorts of imaginative efforts. The reality was ecumenical and interfaith, although the central energy seemed to be in the Protestant Mainline groups.

John Fletcher had just begun exploring an effort to invent a totally new institution for the education of leaders of religious congregations— an effort that was to be based on engaging the leaders in the life of the congregation, learning where they worked. He attracted a remarkable group of educators, both lay and clergy, in churches and synagogues. People like Verna Dozier and Parker Palmer. The work resonated with many in the philanthropic world, especially the Lilly Endowment, and sparks moved back and forth with others in theological education, especially Bill Webber at New York Theological Seminary.

The whole approach to education was in ferment. St. Mark's Episcopal Church was deep into the second decade of its exploration of Functional Education ("Func Ed") as pioneered by Charles Penniman of St. Louis and the Education Center there. James Adams, rector of St. Mark's, and Celia Hahn were leading new ways of conceiving the work of education in congregations.

Gordon and Mary Cosby and Elizabeth O'Connor and their colleagues had begun the remarkable ministry of the Church of the Savior with its New Testament model of Christian life as a "journey inward; journey outward."

John Denham had brought together a network of pastors and educators in the Mid-Atlantic Training Committee (MATC), which fielded a wide curriculum of leadership education across the area from Delaware to the Carolinas. In time, hundreds of lay and clergy leaders were being trained in the practical use of the behavioral sciences and group life. Many denominations provided leaders and participants.

James Anderson, John Harris, and Jeanne Haldane, staff persons for the Episcopal Dioceses of Washington and Maryland, had begun collaborating on aiding local congregations and clergy, and were using the technologies of organizational development. They invented new ways for clergy to be assisted to become collaborative leaders of teams instead of autocrats.

Clinical Pastoral Education was a strong influence, led by work of Ernie Bruder at St. Elizabeth's Hospital and Knox Kreutzer at Lorton Reformatory. The whole world of psychological study was actively engaged in the thinking. Not seen at that time visibly, but beginning and increasing in importance, was the work of Murray Bowen at Georgetown, work that later became known as family systems theory and Practice. Ed Friedman, a remarkable local rabbi, became mentor for a group of particularly influential clergy, helping family systems become a staple resource for clergy across the country.

Ted and Cynthia Wedel—he as warden of the College of Preachers and she as leader of volunteers and later as vice president of the World Council of Churches—led major efforts at education of clergy and laity across the country in the behavioral sciences. Their work fed into and from the work of Reuel Howe at Virginia Seminary.

That, then, was something of the mix the Alban Institute found itself among in 1974. Looked at now, with a view from nearly half a century later, one wonders if it might not have been some kind of a desperate flowering of possibilities cast up by reactions to a century of ghastly wars. A flowering that was also a foreshadowing of darker, more difficult times being born.

But, with the vision we had then, what did we do?

At the time we did what we had come to think worked. We gathered ideas and the people with ideas, we shaped ideas into goals and designed ways of achieving them, and then we set out to accomplish our goals.

In ordinary language, we developed proposals and took them to philanthropic foundations for the resources that would make it possible for us to do all of that.

The characteristic response of the foundations was to cherry-pick the proposals they had received and allocate their resources toward the most promising. Soon, with much experience of the endless ability of that world to produce a plethora of good ideas and a vast group of passionate advocates for this goal or that, foundations began to set limits. On proposals. And especially on permanence.

The standard became to give two- or three-year grants only, with full funding the first year, two-thirds funding the second year, and one-third funding in the third and final year. Why? So that the proposal-seekers would themselves secure one-third funding by the second year, two-thirds by the third, and be fully funded by the next year.

It almost never worked. The world is full of the agencies with admirable ideas, imaginative plans, and pioneering launches that soon crashed to the ground ignominiously. The world is full of people of enormous energy and creativity that I knew in their prime. People wandering the world of institutions today with a vacant look in their eyes; people who are known for the incredibly exciting ideas they invented, wondering where it all went. Somehow the promises, the hope, just evaporated.

Everybody *thought* that was the way to get something going in those heady days, but we were wrong. Of the ones I mentioned above, St. Mark's is still going strong. The Church of the Savior is still going. Neither of them went the way of proposals and philanthropy. We tried to go that way at Alban in the beginning, but the foundation we counted on cut us off—so we had to face a life without an angel.

CHAPTER 12

Chasing Rabbits

We broke a lot of the rules during Project Test Pattern and the early years of the Alban Institute, and I am struggling to tell the story as coherently as I can. The path was not direct and clear, and I have to play loose with the sequential narrative. As we had learned in PTP, we wanted to act on the best knowledge we had, watch carefully what happened, then adjust and move ahead.

But stuff kept interrupting us. We'd start following up hunches but new things would emerge. We'd follow the track of a hunch, and a rabbit would run across the track and lead us to something more promising. Sometimes something we'd left unexplored came back to be the true issue. Sometimes the rabbit that seemed to lead us astray turned out to be the track we needed to follow. We wanted to pay attention to what happened, and adjust what we did to what we learned. Once or twice what we thought was a distracting rabbit turned out to be the true path.

Changing Pastors

One very promising rabbit ran across our track during Project Test Pattern, as we met to figure out what we had learned in our consultations with congregations. The theme we focused on and chased was simple: What goes on when a congregation changes its pastor?[1] Let me walk through what happened as we followed that rabbit—chasing it and the other rabbits that popped up and ran this way and that—and try to describe what happened and what we learned.

I do not know when we in Project Test Pattern and Alban really first focused on this as a big—perhaps *the* big—issue about change in congregations. I think it emerged as common knowledge from our own experiences in congregations as members or teachers or pastors ourselves. We had all experienced change in congregations—sometimes exciting, sometimes awful, sometimes "blah"—when *our* pastor changed. When we asked people about their congregations, they remembered change exactly as we did. They remembered times when they changed pastors as times of *change*:

- "When old Dr. Smith was here, we always . . . ; but when the new pastor came, it all changed."
- "We used to have a great youth program, but when Rev. Johnson came we got all involved with outreach and feeding programs."
- "Preaching was what Sunday was all about until Ms. Black started Bible study groups."
- "We all knew each other in the days when Parson Jones was here; but now-a-days with that new minister it has all changed!"
- "The church was always standing room only when Mr. Allison was here, but now . . . lots of the pews are empty."

"Then" and "now." That's what they remembered. That was our clue. That was how people remembered change.

We knew that was oversimplifying a lot. Changes like that involved a whole lot more—changes in the world outside, changes in the local economy, people moving to town or away—a whole mass of changes influencing them.

But they remembered change in the congregation and, rightly or wrongly, they connected that change with the change of pastors.

In Lewin's theory, we recognized the moment of changing pastors as a moment when the congregation experienced no longer being in equilibrium, in stasis. It was a moment in which everybody realized change had to happen.

This popular perception matched the thinking my associates and I had late in Project Test Pattern, after the first model of the project had collapsed in the first six months and the second was beginning to pay off with more knowledge about congregations and with the consulting process seeming to produce results.

First off, we got clear that we *were* actually getting useful results in parishes. But we were also coming to understand that the change we were getting was hard, required really talented (and consequently expensive) consultants, demanded congregations that were serious about changing, and took a lot of time. As a way to learn parish dynamics and as a way to address serious problems in a congregation, our method had promise. However, as a strategy for facilitating a major retooling of congregations, we felt we were barking up the wrong tree. The method had promise for *some* parishes—although not necessarily many of them—but it was hard, took time and expertise, and was consequently expensive. It *worked*, but it was not a practical way to turn lots of parishes around.

One of us somehow came up with an analogy: What we had discovered for parishes was analogous to psychoanalysis for healing a damaged person. With the right psychoanalyst and with the right patient, and with a long period of work and the investment of a lot of money, we all knew of some people who were truly transformed. But it was a dicey business—in many cases, for many reasons, it simply didn't work.

To treat one patient was difficult, costly, and long. Psychoanalysis was a great tool for some persons, sometimes a magical tool, and it also developed new insights and knowledge for the rest of us. But it was not a practical strategy for changing community mental health. Similarly, the process of parish consultation held real promise for some situations; but as a strategy for renewal of congregations across the churches, it was probably a nonstarter.

On the other hand, we realized that if we could isolate consultation as a tool for learning, and could focus that learning at a particularly open moment in the congregation's life, we just might be able to find a way to affect many congregations and move them toward creative change.

Bingo! The moment when one pastor left and another came was one every congregation went through periodically. If we could focus the technology of parish consultation on that strategic moment of pastoral change, we might discover resources that could be used on a broad basis to strengthen parish ministry.

That is exactly what we set out to do in the final year of Project Test Pattern. On top of wrapping up the consultations we had begun, and collecting all the knowledge we could from that effort, we designed a process for targeting the use of consultation in congregations undergoing pastoral change.

We built on what we had already learned. We decided that the local option mattered: The congregation would have the choice to join the process or not. We decided to recruit twelve dioceses, asking their bishops to offer every congregation that was seeking a new pastor the option of using a consultant to help them with the search process. The process would last for just six months, since we were in no position to offer a long-term commitment. Congregations were not required to use a consultant—they could follow the usual search method if they preferred—but the bishop would encourage them to use the consultant.

We in the project would take on the task of working with a consultant of the bishop's choosing, with the understanding that the consultant would be willing to share what happened and what they learned. We would also get agreements with the bishop to allow us to send someone to the congregation *after* the new pastor was in place to talk to people in the parish and the new pastor about how it had gone.

There was more. We did have a larger commitment to improve things, to strategically act to strengthen congregations through this intervention. We hoped to change the norms of the church so that using consultation regularly in the pastoral change process would become normative in the church. We named that as a goal.

So we strategically chose bishops with that in mind. We knew how the House of Bishops operated, and we had no stake in passing rules or ordinances. We wanted to change normative behavior at that change point. Conversation and exchange of ideas and experience was the House's way of business. So we chose bishops whose voices were respected, bishops from dioceses across the country, bishops representing conservative and liberal constituencies, bishops who listened to others and were not felt to be hide-bound. To be honest, bishops other bishops seemed to trust.

Would it work or would it bomb?

The first signal was that the bishops bought in. All twelve. As the project continued, we got data from all but two of them. The data coming in was thinner than in the earlier consultations (we had no direct contract with the consultants the bishops used, and some were more forthcoming than others, plus they did not operate in teams, but as individuals). The field trips we made to the places where the consultations had happened were most productive, however. All the data went to Bill Yon, a project associate in Alabama, and to Celia Hahn in our office. Bill produced a monograph from those reports that was published just as Project Test Pattern ended: *Prime Time for Renewal*. Celia Hahn produced a book for wider circulation, *The Minister Is Leaving*. Its manuscript went to the publisher on the last day of PTP, and it was published by Seabury Press later in 1974. Both publications were widely used.

The second signal was unexpected. We had asked the twelve bishops to try the method for six months. At the end of the six months, they kept on using the same method, because apparently it had sold itself to them. We suspected that we had influenced the norms about working on change of pastors. In fact, they did something we had only hoped for. Those bishops, having been sold on the approach, told others about it, and it was picked up in other places. We did not control the use of the process, but we were glad to see it spread. We discovered, to our surprise, that some of the other denominations discovered the method and either copied or adapted it to their use.[2]

Meanwhile another rabbit ran across our track. We had found the "open" moment for the parish that was "in between" senior pastors, but also it pointed to another dimension of change, backed up by other data we received.

John Fletcher's study of what laypeople expected of clergy pointed to an unusual fact: In many effective clergy-lay pastoral relationships there were often periods when physical illness of the clergyperson required a lengthy absence or reduced engagement. Sometimes it was a minor illness that simply would not heal; in other cases family problems or a period of depression effectively removed the clergyperson from full-time effectiveness. Sometimes, Fletcher discovered, this period of forced withdrawal actually seemed to precipitate a new time of increased, but deeper, effectiveness.[3]

A similar piece of evidence came in a book Alban put together (*Learning to Share the Ministry* by James Adams and Celia Hahn) to describe how St. Mark's Church in Washington, DC, faced a prolonged separation from their pastor during a sabbatical.

In both these two instances and some other anecdotes that came to our attention, we began to smell another reality—that whenever the designated leader of the religious community is away, the whole issue of how lay and clergy relate in leadership comes into creative conversation. Indeed, the larger issue of clericalism in the church is potentially at play here—the fact that many see religious organizations dominated by the leadership of ordained persons, although New Testament images point toward a wider ministry of the laity.

Although Project Test Pattern of The Episcopal Church played out its life, those learnings about changing pastors turned into key pieces of the agenda for the early life of the Alban Institute.

Unfinished Business

When my Alban advisors gathered to deal with life after our close brush with death, we complained and worried and tried to figure out what to do next. Having done our bitching and crying, we got down to business. I think it was Jack who spoke up first: "How about our unfinished business?" he asked. "What about what happens to the pastor who starts up after all the folderol about 'calling,' and 'search,' and 'appointment'?"

Jim picked it up there: "What about the ones who crash and burn? We hear a lot about that. And a lot of those we tracked in the vacancy research followed somebody who had actually crashed before. What about all that? Could we help people understand the process of starting up so as to avoid some of the trauma that goes on when a pastorate turns sour?"

The board stuck with me. Indeed, we pushed ahead with some plans for publishing and for more research on that issue. We began interviews with newly appointed or selected clergy to learn the dynamics of those first six to twelve months in the new job.

By the end of that year, we had pushed ahead on our research into how pastors can start a new job, and because of the shortage of finances we even invented a new model of research—one I came to call the "Tom Sawyer Fence-Painting Model." We charged people to teach us what they knew. Not just any people, but people who knew stuff but didn't know they knew it. For example, we knew how United Methodists handle pastor change, having a "changing pulpit day" each June. On the same day, all the pastors who were changing parishes made their change. This happened every year. So we had a captive audience of people that first week in June, all of whom were changing parishes, most of whom had done so several times already, and we knew what questions to ask them. We also knew some things about changing that most of them had never reflected on.

So, in total audacity, we offered to do a conference to help the pastors making a change spend time reflecting on what they had already learned and also to address issues we knew to be important whether or not they had already reflected on them. Each of them came out of the conference clearer and more skillful in making the change, and we came out with remarkable new stores of knowledge from able people who had learned it the hard way.

Tom Sawyer and Becky came away not just with a newly white-washed fence, but also with all sorts of things the volunteer painters had given them for the privilege of painting. We got our expenses and fees paid by the conference for letting us pick their brains. We got paid and they got skills in learning from their experience.

As with the Methodists, so with the Army chaplains. Chaplains also changed jobs at least every three years, and we got to work with them about their change experience at Fort Campbell, Kentucky. Again, we knew enough to help them change, but we also went to school on how they had experienced the change. We discovered how much raw wisdom many of those pastors had, but they had never had a chance to reflect on or identify what they knew. Again, we were paid, but we also learned as much or more than they did.[4]

What did I learn? That lots of capable people in lots of congregations changed jobs regularly. That they often had stores of helpful knowledge about how to do it and what caused problems. Almost never had they been asked to reflect on what they had learned and almost nobody in the denominational systems themselves had many clues about what led to creative ministries and what led the opposite way. And that it was possible to help launch more constructive pastoral ministry by reflecting on what worked and what didn't and by sharing that knowledge with those to start a new pastorate.

We also learned, unhappily, that most judicatories and national church staffs were so overloaded with tasks to be carried out that they had little or no time or energy with which to help local pastors reflect on the large amount of learnings in their experience.

By early 1975, Roy Oswald, a Lutheran now working part-time with us, was able to produce a most helpful monograph on what we had learned: *The Pastor as Newcomer*. Although we had no money for printing costs, I had located a congregation in New Jersey that made small grants, and they funded the printing.

We started with nothing. But we found that many of the clergy and laity in the churches had storehouses of experience, wisdom, and helpful knowledge. We found that church systems could and would pay if their clergy got help in making better transitions. So we could generate income by helping congregations and pastors get off to better experiences with each other, and we could also sell written assistance to those who could not come to our training events.

In the process, we also got clues about how to work in the new world we had stumbled into. What I did not know was how hungry clergy and congregations were for the kind of practical knowledge we were digging up. Our monographs sold. And we survived. Groups asked us to come teach what we had learned. We continued to discover people who had useful knowledge we could gather, print, and pass along.

And that's when we realized another rabbit had already run across out track, and we had not recognized it.

CHAPTER 13

In the Interim

I was walking by my office one morning when Felix Kloman, a retired Episcopal pastor, called to me across the street (Wisconsin Avenue, for those who need to know).[1] "Loren," he said, "what are you going to do about Craig Eder?" I knew Craig. He was also a retired clergyman who, after a distinguished career as chaplain of a boy's school, had taken up a practice of becoming *locum tenens* and served in parishes where the previous pastor had retired or died or was otherwise elsewhere for a while (or permanently, as the case might be).

"What do you mean?" was my reply, because I didn't have any idea what he meant.

"He's really doing a great job out at St. Somebody's Church in suburban Maryland. We need more people like that!"

"What do you want me to do?" I asked Felix.

"We need people like that," he said. "Smart people, good pastors to put in all the parishes we have in the church who are changing pastors in the next year or so. Lots of those parishes really need extra care, and we need more Craig Eders."

Over a cup of coffee later, he elaborated. "St. Swithin's in Georgetown has gone through a civil war, and there is blood all over the walls—they need somebody to come clean up the wreckage and get some healing done before they send in a long-term pastor. Maybe six months or a year. And you know Dr. Johnson is retiring at Holy Smoke parish after forty-five years as rector. Those people are going to need some grief work as well as help on how to work with a stranger pastor!"

I got the point and added my own, "There's also All Saints'—that staff of four clergy are likely to kill each other to get the job—they really need somebody to come in, maybe just as a referee, and that place is so complex!"

We sort of agreed about the issue, which was when I remembered the rabbit that had already run across our path: Keith Irwin. Keith had come to me a couple of years earlier when I realized we were going to need more people trained to be parish consultants. He was a Presbyterian; I think he got to me because he was close to Robbie MacFarlane, who had been an advisor to Project Test Pattern. He asked to get into the MATC consultant training program because he thought those skills would be useful to him in a job he had taken in South Dakota.[2]

That all turned out to be the beginning of the Interim Pastorate! Of course it was just a germ. But that was the beginning.

The key thing, though, is *how* it all started. Not as a "plan," but by listening, observing, and connecting people, things, and ideas.

A lot of work had to follow, and all along we had to sweat out how to pay for it. We talked to people, looked around for resource people, and tried to find church executives who might want to be involved. I located a small pot of money when I connected with Buck Patton, a neat lay leader of a Congregational church in Columbus who had a family foundation and who was willing to be tapped for about $7,000 to put together a meeting of those interested in the idea.

We pulled together a staff that knew how to listen and ask good questions and contracted with a conference center in St. Louis. We worked to get executives of the Lutherans (representing three of the Lutheran bodies of the time), Presbyterians, Unitarian-Universalists, Episcopalians, United Congregationalists, Disciples of Christ, and I don't remember who else to agree to come together to learn and think. We also found about eighteen people like Craig Eder (including Craig himself as well as Keith Irwin) to be our guinea pigs, telling what they did and how. And John Denham, head of the training group with whom we had conspired to spin off the training of consultants, was there. I had come to suspect we might need to train people to do this kind of skilled ministry between pastors. Roy Oswald came along as core staff with me.

That's the beginning. It took off. Some writing followed, but everybody just saw right away that this was an important step for us all. All the denominations had ways of providing pastoral help during pastoral change, but most of what existed amounted to a sort of baby-sitting. Keith, Craig, the staff, and I brought a real upgrade to the quality and skills needed in the "interim," as we had begun to call it.[3]

We got surprises too. People interested in interim pastorates were not all like Craig and Keith. First—a lot of very able clergy who were not at or near retirement had found a challenging ministry in this interim period already. Some of them just liked to move from things frequently. One had another job as a hunting-fishing guide and didn't want to work more than six or eight months of the year as a pastor. Some had just learned they weren't good at staying put—they liked and were good at short-term, sometimes intense work; but after a half year or year they were tired of the job and the people were tired of them. Another anomaly—several of these denominations were in the early stages of having many women seeking pastoral assignments, and congregations were unsure of making such a change from a male to a female pastor. Women interims were a strategy some denominations and their women candidates began to see as a way to help such congregations and denominations make some moves.

We had been right about the strategic importance of the interim in strengthening congregational life, and had developed one helpful technology—organizational development consultation. Having found it a helpful tool—but an inadequate strategy for widespread use—we spun off training consultants to a training institution. We then adapted consultation for use at a more strategic moment, the change of pastors. We had tested both in PTP, while developing ways to capture and publish what had been learned for wider use.

At the Alban Institute we identified another strategic form of intervention, interim consultation, resulting in the development of a new role, that of the professional interim pastor. Feedback from early interim pastors helped us identify our next issue—those who served as interim pastors had little support. Their denominational systems often did not understand the tensions they lived with: the need periodically to change jobs, with no steady income or permanent place to live; the lack of understanding of their kind of ministry by other pastors and laity; the moves from place to place that took them out of connection with colleagues.

As the use of interim pastors grew, the need for a profession network of their own became clear. Roy and I, along with Rip Coffin and

Ralph Macy, two such pastors, wanted to make that happen. We knew it should be an ecumenical network, since there were too few interim pastors in any one denomination and they were scattered all around the country. Going back to Buck Patton for help, we got enough money to subsidize annual meetings of interim pastors for two years, which was enough for them—since they were well aware of their need—to form a professional network.

In the beginning, the network proposed to become a subsidiary of the Alban Institute, but Alban pushed, and they at first reluctantly, later with great enthusiasm, chose independence. The Interim Ministry Network has become a strong, independent institution that now has had over thirty annual meetings. An unexpected outcome was that several of the denominations did develop large enough groups of interim pastors to start smaller denominational networks, which now meet in conjunction with the national Interim Ministry Network.

I have gone on for a number of pages about one group of interventions we were called on to initiate and nurture in religious institutions—all connected to the processes by which pastoral leadership in the local congregation changes from one pastor to another. We worked primarily with denominational systems in which the members of the local congregation had a primary voice in the selection of the new pastor. In such situations we used the language of "calling." The congregation calls the pastor into leadership. Other denominations use different ways of making this decision through a form of executive authority—there we use the language of "appointment." Either a bishop or another authorized person or group makes the leadership decision for the congregation, sometimes after consultation with some members of the congregation. We found that many of those in the appointment camp found our work clarifying the dynamics of the change helpful, and that the learnings about start-up were easily applicable there. Those in the calling camp incorporated both into their processes.

But gradually, as Alban learned more, the issues of changing pastors became less central to our work. More and more of the ordinary work shifted into the denominational networks as workshops and publications expanded the availability of the knowledge and methods we had developed.

That felt healthy to me. We encouraged others to take and adapt our learnings to their own systems.

CHAPTER 14

Let's Talk about Money

One morning I got a phone call from a stranger in Connecticut, a pastor in a parish of the United Church of Christ. "Loren," he said to me, "I've heard you help new pastors connect with a new job."

Assuming he was talking about our work on pastorate start-ups, I said, "Well, John," I had picked up his name from the operator, "we do know something about that; what can I help you with?" I figured I could at least sell him a couple of monographs!

"Well, Loren," he continued, "I got into this congregation about three or four months ago, and I keep getting confused!"

"What's the issue?" I asked him.

"It smells as if there's a lot of money around here, but I can't find it!" he elaborated.

I began to smell something I'd run into before. The way churches and all sorts of religious institutions fuzz things up when they talk about money. They hide stuff. Refuse to talk straight. It's as if they are either stupid or allergic whenever people bring "money," or "budgets," or "finances" into the conversation. I asked a few questions, and it was clear that there really were some trust funds or sources of money flow that the pastor simply had no knowledge of, yet he was responsible for the life of the congregation.

I was sensitive to the issue because I *did* try to raise money from parishes, and I'd found myself usually trashed by wealthy congregations. I was made to feel like I had to take my hat off and go to the back door. Foundations were often equally bad—they really were often unaware of the arrogance with which they treated people seeking grants. I had found that some foundations (but *very* few wealthy congregations) were different—instead of projecting their need to protect the money from unscrupulous people trying to steal it, they realized they had a responsibility to look for opportunities to use their funds for imaginative possibilities. They were looking for ways to invest their funds in things they believed in, and that was a very different approach from the norm.

I had run into the opposite problem several times too—a congregation where someone who is thought to be a financial expert gets all sorts of power in the congregation, wheeling and dealing with confidence, and intimidating members, who shut up and back down in dealing with him or her. Lots of parish crises are brought on by people who are loud and assertive and even unpleasant. Others simply do not want to tangle with them.

I was, therefore, aware that money was often a problem for congregations, and this looked like a good opportunity to explore that.

In this case I called on a member of my board, Fletcher Lutz, to take a few days to go see what was going on in that New Haven church. Fletcher was a UCC layperson, the comptroller of a federal agency, and a CPA. He went up to Connecticut and spent three days looking over the parish records and files, and reported back. He found there were six different trusts for that congregation, housed in four different banks and with six different trust statements. Nobody on the board of the congregation knew where the funds were or who was responsible for them. The banks were happy to manage the money since nobody bothered them about it, but they sometimes wondered who should give them directions.

The case had a happy ending. The congregation and the pastor got enough information to begin making better decisions about what their resources actually were and how they were handled. The banks each got clear about what was expected of them. And the pastor began to get a better grip on the life of the congregation.

What I got was even more important. I began to realize two things I simply had not thought about much before: (1) The financial framework of congregations charged with the care of endowment funds was confused and difficult; and (2) boards and clergy were often unprepared for responsible management of such funds.

Unexpectedly, only a couple of months later I got an SOS from a congregation in a small town in Virginia. The tiny church, actually led by a seminary student temporarily because the budget wouldn't support an ordained pastor, had suffered the death of a prominent member, a bachelor who had farmed a large estate left him by his "First Family" progenitors. The farm, valued at $7 million, was left entirely to the local church. The vestry of the parish was made up of truck farmers, storekeepers, and a housewife. Nobody there had a clue about what was needed.[1]

Once again, I saw something because I was outside the silo the people in those two congregations were in. They were stuck until they got input from outside their own local situation.

It was about then that Eli Lilly's estate was settled. Lilly had been a lifelong member of Christ Church in Indianapolis, and he had been generous to churches and agencies all his life. In his estate he left large sums to three of the Episcopal Churches on Meridian Street in his hometown. This was not his first gift to those churches, which already had modest endowments, but the new gifts made the endowments significantly larger.

An idea had been growing in me ever since the first serendipitous call from Connecticut. Churches with significant endowments actually had issues other congregations did not have, and they often did not have people with experience dealing with large sums of money.

In my short and inadequate history of all this, I had already run into issues that seemed to paralyze some of them. First, there was the fight: "Money is bad—we ought to give it away right now" vs. "John asked us to be trustees of his money and continue to use it after his death for things the church stands for—it's our responsibility!" Then, there was the problem most churches had never come up against: conflict of interest. A church member, the local banker, says, "Listen, I manage money professionally all the time. Give it to the care of my bank—we'll invest it for you, give you monthly reports, and make sure it's there when you need it. Meanwhile, we'll pay you 2 percent every year." How do you turn down such a generous offer from a church member? Or another who is an investment adviser who offers to manage the corpus and build up the capital. How do you decide whether that is a good idea or not?

Along about then I ran across a dissertation from a pastor in Connecticut (I got a lot of such dissertations from clergy in Doctor of Ministry courses who were hoping to get published). It was the story of an endowment that had been given—$600,000 as I remember it—in about 1950 (it was then about 1985). The dissertation told how much the congregation had accomplished with the income from the gift (things like a major rebuilding of the parish kitchen; helping buy a new fire engine for the town; funding the start-up and operation of a large Meals on Wheels program in the county—quite a few substantive projects). But the dissertation ended with great pleasure with the statement that their proudest accomplishment was to have done all that, and the endowment in 1985 had only declined by about $100,000. I'm no mathematician, but I saw the flaw in that one—if they had been responsible with their $600,000, in those years of economic growth, they should at least have increased their capital two or three times to assure continuing ability to do the kind of outreach the original grant had supported. A congregation with an endowment needed to have a mind-set about maintaining its ability to serve, not degrading it.[2]

The three churches in Indianapolis put the issue before me, because I was doing a lot of work with one of them. I said to the pastor, "Next time I'm in Indianapolis, I'd love to have lunch with the three clergy." He agreed with me and set up a meeting.

When the four of us were together at the table, I raised the question that had come to me: "I think churches that have sizeable endowments have problems other churches don't have; they also have opportunities other churches don't have; they have issues to deal with that other churches don't have. I think it would be a good thing if leaders of such congregations had opportunities to get together to work on those things. And I think the three of you, because you know something about the issue and because you are at a new starting point—you might be the ones who could launch such an effort."

They bought the idea, checked it out with colleagues in similar congregations, and planned several meetings to work over the idea. One critical piece they decided needed to be there from the beginning: The meetings needed to include several lay leaders from each congregation; Clergy alone could not come.

From the first meeting, I charged them a fee for my time. That is what I always did. I did it, frankly, to put bread on the table at my house—to keep the institute alive and me in my job. I did not know how important it was for other reasons. It forced these few, and gradually more, congregations to have a budget and to figure out a way to pay for what they wanted to do. It wasn't an enormous amount, but not peanuts, either. From the beginning the people backing the idea took on the responsibility of paying for it and collaborating with others to pay.

For our first gathering—we called it our "Come to Jesus meeting"—I had put together a budget of what it would cost, by my estimate, for the group to mount a national organization to work with endowed congregations. I think it came to about $75,000. When I put the number on the blackboard, there was a sharp intake of breath. Yes, they wanted to help one another; yes, this was something nobody was doing or would do if they didn't do it; yes, they knew it was important—but by God, why didn't somebody else see the importance and see that it was done? No. Nobody would. Nobody had. It was up to them—put up or shut up. There was a long silence (there were twenty to thirty people in the room who could write a check for that amount; many of them professionally dealt with multiples of that amount all the time). More silence. Then a layman from a church in Kansas City said, "I bet our parish could put up $5,000." And the dam broke. Bob Parks from Trinity, New York, said, "You all do that and I'm sure Trinity can do $7,500." And others piled in. They didn't make my guesstimate, but by the end of the day some $55,000 was pledged, and the decision was "Go!"

The next meeting was at the College of Preachers at the National Cathedral, with some twenty-three or twenty-four congregations present—all with a rector and two or three key lay leaders (many of whom knew each other from court cases or written papers or reputation, but most of whom had never recognized the church connection with the others). Bob Parks saw me bringing the group together and said, "What are you doing here, Loren? Looks to me like we have the fox looking out for the chickens!" He realized, as did many in the meeting, that I *was* a fundraiser for the Alban Institute and that I *did* charge fees for my time—but that this was another matter.

In fact, that gathering was a major step in the group's growth into what subsequently became one of the strongest independent groups in The Episcopal Church, one whose annual meetings bring together a remarkable group of vital congregations with others trying to learn how to be more creative with their financial strength.

As I worked with the Consortium of Endowed Episcopal Parishes, I wondered about the other endowed parishes. Tom Stewart was pastor of Westminster Presbyterian congregation in Buffalo, New York. Because his parish had an endowment, he asked me about what the Episcopalians were doing. With the permission of the consortium,

I asked him to come to several of their meetings, and he got the idea of replicating that effort in his denomination. Bob Lynn at the Lilly Endowment had also heard of the work and arranged a grant that funded some of my time to work with other denominations. I did so with several, but all of them had serious difficulty making the step of taking responsibility for their life—paying the bill for doing something different.

The Presbyterian effort resulted in a series of annual meetings, and finally a new structure: the PEER (Presbyterian Endowment Education Resource) Network, which still works on these issues, partially supported by the Presbyterian Foundation. The Lutherans fielded a strong group of endowed parishes, but never solved the problem of taking financial responsibility for their own life. It no longer exists. Similar efforts began, but faded, in the United Church of Christ, the Unitarian Universalist Association, and the United Methodist Church.

I've reflected on the experience with those congregations. One learning is explicit in what I've said. It is critical for a group of congregations that wants to make a difference and face something that is not on the denominational agenda to do two things: (1) Take responsibility for generating the funds needed to make it happen; and (2) achieve "critical mass," by which I mean a large enough membership to give the group a sense of strength and ability.

We also learned that it is difficult in religious community, at least in America, to talk straight about money. Almost all our meetings began with confession—confession in public about where the money came from and what they used it for. It was an experience we had not expected to be so important, but it put everybody on the same ground. It was, for these congregational leaders, emotionally analogous to an alcoholic admitting his or her alcoholism. I am not comfortable about what that says about church membership and the meaning of money in our society.

One other thing this experience taught me about people and churches. You see, my hope was to form one ecumenical group of parishes to face this together. I think I learned that people do not "think" ecumenically; they think denominationally. Is it a matter of trust? Of comfort? I don't know. But parish leaders could talk about this challenging material with others of their own denomination, but were not attracted to doing so with those of other groups.

CHAPTER 15

Expanding the Conversation

His name was Carl Dudley. He walked into my office at the National Cathedral unannounced. He'd heard about the Alban Institute and our commitment to congregations. He was teaching at McCormick Theological Seminary in Chicago. I knew the seminary because a guy named Bob Worley was there, and he was working with consultants in congregations and beginning to develop a seminary course in "organizational development." Sounded something like what we had tried in PTP.

I liked Carl right away, and the conversation just flew. He was headed home from a conference about small congregations that Hartford Seminary had sponsored. He showed me a paper: the script for a speech he'd been asked to give up there. I scanned it, gulped, and then read it. My response? Wow! "Carl, this is fantastic. I never saw this sort of stuff. People need to see it." The title was "The Unique Dynamics of the Small Church."

The long and the short of it was that I asked if we could publish it and he said that we could. I think I paid him the usual fee, $25. We sold barrels of them, and it changed how people understood small church life. Abingdon Press found him and the paper, got him to expand it into a book, which they titled *Making the Small Church Effective*. I've always had a problem with Abingdon for two reasons: (1) They stole that paper from us, and our sales went down the drain, and more importantly (2) the publisher, shooting for sales, totally misrepresented Carl's message in the title. Carl's point was that small churches don't give a rip about "effectiveness."

101

Effectiveness is a characteristic that clergy are in love with and that city folk and suburbanites would die for. But people in small churches aren't interested in it. Plainly, they don't give a damn about it. They want to be a family; they want to care about each other and—yes, at times—to fight with each other. They don't want to "plan," which makes them the bane of young clergy, the only ones except the retired ones who ever get sent there. And bishops and executives only care because they are so much trouble all the time: running out of money before the year is over, not paying their share of the budget, wearing out the young clergy sent to "fix" them. And they resent being "fixed."

Carl had seen that in his own pastorate in St. Louis, but he was the first one to say it out loud. His background in sociology gave him eyes to see stuff others didn't see. We became fast friends, and some thirty or forty years later had several great weekend trips together to see Bob Lynn in retirement in Maine, just to talk.

Bill McKinney was another one we just bumped into. Another sociologist. I found him in a UCC judicatory office, but he quickly got snatched up for their national headquarters in Cleveland. I met him when Carl and I were on another trip to understand congregations. With what we came to call the "Gang of Five," we had designed a case study and hired Bob and Alice Evans to be the writers. As we struggled with the Evanses preliminary work, it was obvious that either we or the Evanses had misperceived what we needed. Everybody pussyfooted around the problem for an hour, and then Bill shot from the hip: "Listen. This work is wrong. It won't do. It's not what we need! Are you willing to listen to us and do what we need?" It worked. Pussyfooting was simply wasting everybody's time. They heard, they could do it, and they wanted to do it. I liked his style, and his ability to be direct continued for the forty or fifty years we've worked together.

Barbara Wheeler snuck up on us. Her quiet demeanor hid the daggers she had behind her skirt. She was the iron lady who led Auburn Seminary (the Presbyterian adjunct to Union Seminary in New York) when few women had even been considered for seminary faculties. I ran into her when a bunch of us were recruited by Warren Deem for a consulting job at Scarritt College in Nashville, a Methodist school that had allowed itself to veer too close to the cliff's edge and faced collapse. Barbara was sharp. Razor sharp. But all that was part-cover for a streak of sweetness and a raucous sense of humor. She and Bill kept us on the subject and made us cut to the chase. More than we wanted to. Several of us came because we'd known Warren when he was consulting with Hartford Seminary about the revolution in theological education they were hatching up there.

Jack Carroll was another sociologist, a Methodist. I forget how he came to us, although I'd known him from South Carolina—he was from the Piedmont and I was from the coastal plain. Jack kept us in touch with the professional academic world, wrote books, and felt guilty when he wasn't working.

I was, well, me. The "me" you've already met in this book. The five of us came together at a meeting in Indianapolis. (Where else? As Willie Hutton said when asked why he kept robbing banks: "That's where they keep the money, isn't it?" He referred to banks; we refer to the Lilly Endowment.) Bob Lynn at Lilly knew we all had a bug about local congregations. He had somebody he wanted us to meet.

That was Jim Hopewell. He'd been at Hartford, but was just back from a sabbatical he'd spent visiting country churches in north Georgia. He had a background in overseas mission, had his doctorate in anthropology, and had started trying to understand congregations in terms of anthropology and Greek mythology. Don't ask me why. He just did. And he wrote a bunch of stories of those small congregations, "reading" them through Greek mythology *and* anthropology.

I'd read a couple of the stories, and Bob wanted us to discuss what Jim had done. I thought it was a classic boondoggle and wouldn't have gone if it hadn't been Lilly calling—I mean I didn't want to make enemies at the only place I *might* be able to get a grant from. I'm not stupid.

I think there were about twelve of us there. The discussion was, well, inconclusive. That's a lie. Jim was pretty silent, and there were ten of us who told him how useless and stupid his papers were. He slumped a bit, and there was an awkward silence. Barbara then said, "You know? It's interesting. I don't think anybody here is taken with these stories, but you know what?" Relieved not to have to stab Jim one more time, I think it was me who said, "What, Barbara?"

She said, "We all criticized the stories, but everybody criticized them for something different!" (That's what I mean about her having daggers behind her skirt!) Pow. We saw it. Each one of us came from a different place in looking at what Jim had seen and told us about!

We started making a list of all the people we knew who were doing work on congregations. Bruce Reed in London. Paul Diettrich in Chicago. Lyle Schaller in Elkhart. We came up with over fifty names. None of us had realized how many people there were, all around the country, focusing their energy on local congregations. Then and there a project got born and a group formed: the Congregational Studies Group. Early on it was the "Gang of Five"—Carl, Bill, Jack, Barbara, and me. We were loose about numbers, and soon several others were added. Once we even had a T-shirt for one of our meetings: "The Gang of Five."

After the meeting in Indianapolis, we conceived of following up by trying to understand the different perspectives that were being used by the people who studied congregations. Eventually we came up with 150 people. We asked them to share their "tools" for looking at congregations, and the Alban Institute published them as *The Whole Church Catalog: Where to Get Tools for Congregational Study and Intervention.* Jim Hopewell read through the whole thing and sorted it out into the four areas we used for several years as the facets to look at when studying congregations: (1) identity; (2) context; (3) process; and (4) program. These four, we believed, covered the different ways these 150 people looked at or studied the congregations with which they worked.

Having identified those four facets, the team decided to get specialists in each of those areas to study one congregation in those four ways, using the professional tools required for each (identity—anthropological; context—sociological; process—organizational analysis; program—evaluation).

The decision was made for trained case writers to do the study, backed up by professionals in each area who would assign the case writers to cover specific areas.

The case was written (with Bill McKinney's outburst described above along the way), and we made a decision to have a public conclave in Atlanta for anybody interested in congregations. We felt excited at what we had learned, but we were not optimistic about who would show up.

We were floored when over three hundred people paid to come to the conference (I was the one who pushed the group to charge a fee, remembering what I had learned from Lewin and had experienced in PTP). The team met afterward and made further plans—to publish the case and the papers written about it[1] and to publish a workbook for seminaries and others who might want to use or communicate our approach.

We did a lot of work putting together that workbook, *Handbook for Congregational Studies*.[2] One major part of that work was holding a seminar at Auburn Seminary for bishops, church executives, and teachers to test the material we had gathered. Shortly after that event, I left the task force, but I have appreciated the raft of books they have spawned, beginning with Barbara Wheeler's edition of Jim Hopewell's book, *Congregation: Stories and Structures*.[3] Jim, who was hit hard with cancer during our work, died shortly after the amazing show he put on at Auburn, teaching his theories and work in an incredible theological ballet. Nobody who saw it has forgotten it.

I left the task force for two reasons: (1) Alban and I couldn't afford it—other members were on salaries and had their expenses paid from budgets, while I had to generate my salary and expenses from my consulting fees at Alban; and (2) when the group chose a publisher for *Handbook for Congregational Studies*, the decision, which I came to agree with, was to have it done by Abingdon, not Alban. I couldn't justify the continuing costs, and I knew the work of studying congregations would go on.

My final formal connection to the task force was a request, since they did not plan to continue educational events, to allow Alban to put on an annual conference for bishops and executives who supervised or worked with multiple congregations. The Alban Institute's Leadership Institute for Bishops and Executives became an important staple in Alban's calendar for a decade. It was also a venue in which we were able to explore other areas of congregational life: conflict, managing clergy violations of sexual boundaries, and many others.

CHAPTER 16

Silos, and What's Wrong with Silos

I have already mentioned the problem we ran into with the way churches were "siloed," as I called it. Now I want to describe two of the silos we ran into, how we worked with them, and how we at least partially found ways to pierce them. The first has to do with that particular fascination that broke out in the churches during the 1960s and 1970s—the silo we called church growth.

The Church Growth Silo

Donald MacGavran is a name of honor in the churches. A prominent missiologist, he was born in India at the end of the nineteenth century and is known for his research and teaching about how a church grows its membership. His work sensitized the churches to the issue of church growth and led to the whole field of church growth, as exemplified in the institute founded at Fuller Seminary in Pasadena, California.[1]

The increasing interest in his studies and work coincided with a marginal sense of "dis-ease" within the Mainline denominations, many of which began to find disturbing signs that the churches that had grown phenomenally in the 1940s and 1950s were finding fewer and fewer members as the sixties turned to the seventies. It was this uneasiness—probably at least partly because the Baby Boom had peaked and was declining—that led Episcopal bishops to come up with the idea for Project Test Pattern. Different people in different places began to notice that something had changed.

106

During those years I was beating the bushes for opportunities to work with individual congregations, groups of clergy, and occasional denominational task forces for fees, trying to keep the Alban Institute alive and solvent. Some contracts, to tell the truth, were not so much intended for learning as for earning. I had learned the skills of a consultant, but I also had the instincts of somebody who wants to understand churches and clergy and judicatories and how they can work better.

I worked where I could find work, but I tried to store up what I saw. And during that time, I saw a lot of similar things. In New England, especially, I saw very large church buildings in the middle of midsized communities. These churches—Presbyterian, United Church of Christ, United Methodist, Episcopal, or other—needed help because their heating bills had hit the ceiling. Middle East crises had sent oil prices through the roof. Heating bills for those large, often-stone buildings had doubled, then doubled again. Winter winds whistled through their stained-glass window frames. Simultaneously, parish members realized that buildings that had been designed for 800 or 1,000 or more members had declined to the point that perhaps only 100 or 150 were in church on Sundays.

Almost every congregation faced a crisis: financial, yes, but it was also personal for the members who remained. The church they loved and the community that had nurtured them felt fragmented and seemed to lose energy. Many churches recognized the crisis and did their best to meet it. They raised money; they repaired leaky windows and weather-stripped the doors or switched from oil to gas furnaces. They instituted membership drives and learned to look for ways to attract new residents, often finding that the new neighbors were of other races, nationalities, and religions. They also cut staff and deferred maintenance.

This was a boom time for people like me, charging fees to help them define their problems and organize themselves to cope better. The church fad salesmen had a field day flogging "new approaches" and "keys to a growing church" programs.

One of my contracts was with the Presbyterian Synod of New England, helping them try to figure out how better to install pastors in their many very small congregations. We were doing all we could, when my colleague up there, Marianne Rhebergen, told me in frustration one day, "It seems hopeless to me! Last year's synod statistics showed how many members we have lost. It was awful!" "What do you mean?" I asked her. "Well," she said, "the synod put together a paper about membership over the past decade, and it said we had lost 29 percent of our members between 1965 and 1975!"

Lights started to go on. Every congregation was in crisis and facing the crisis alone. But nobody was paying attention to the framework of crisis we were in, all together. I started thinking about the Lutherans I had worked with in Connecticut, the Episcopalians in Rhode Island, and the American Baptists in New York State.

Because everybody was siloed, they all felt alone. It was understood to be a local problem by each of them. It was your parish or your diocese that had the problem. No matter that twelve other congregations in the same town were in the same boat. No matter that the Methodists were facing exactly the same thing the Congregationalists were facing. Each group was trying to fix what was going on where they were.

Later, much later, I got an image for what was going on. It was as if a whole bunch of boats were in a shallow harbor, and the tide started going out. Those in each boat were panicking. Some were trying to push their boat through the mud to deeper water; some were throwing heavy stuff overboard; some were giving up and walking to shore; some were praying to find enough water to stay afloat as long as they could. Classic siloing; each facing its own problem, growing more and more hysterical about it. Nobody noticing that there was something going on that was bigger than its silo.

In the beginning I didn't know for sure. It was a hunch. I decided to try to find out if there was anything to it. I didn't feel we had time or money for classic research, worrying about the "validity" of the data and all that stuff. So I went quick and dirty. We didn't have access to the computers needed to crunch the data, but I knew Hartford Seminary did. I knew Jack Carroll there, and that he'd probably go along with me. Tom Stewart, the same guy from Westminister Presbyterian Church who worked with me on endowed churches, had a discretionary fund and could put up several hundred dollars. With Jack, we put together a piece of research we thought would do the job.

Hartford, with its connections across New England, had yearbooks from all the judicatories up there. We dug through those yearbooks for 1970, 1975, and 1980 for whatever comparative statistics we could locate, the things that were just regularly reported every year.

We decided (with some disregard for professional standards of statistical accuracy) to report what they reported on a bunch of things: number of members; number of church school teachers; number of funerals; number of congregations; local expenditures; benevolence expenditures. We *knew* different denominations used different technical terms for some of these things, but we shot for what we could get. We went for data from the five denominations whose records or yearbooks we had: The Lutheran Church in America; The Episcopal Church; the United Church of Christ; the United Methodist Church; the United Presbyterian Church.

Hartford and Alban published a report on the research in 1983.[2] My hunch had been right. We were not dealing with a local problem. We were not dealing with the problem of one denomination, and everybody working their tails off to "fix" the problem was doomed to failure. The problem wasn't a local problem, a problem of one congregation or one denomination. Something new was happening, and it was happening all across the area.

The way we had siloed everything had hidden the truth from us. Nobody was going to fix what was wrong. We had to dig deeper; we had to imagine a lot more than we had; we had to look harder.

I wanted to replicate the study in the other geographical areas of the country, but we never had the time or funds to do so. Actually, we didn't have to; better, more comprehensive studies were done by people with the skills to do them and a flood of books about what was going on came out over the next decade or so. Jack Carroll, Bill McKinney, and David Roozen were involved, as was my old friend from the Panama research project we'd done in North Carolina, Wade Clark Roof.

The Silo of Local Blinders

This silo I ran into in Seattle. I was intrigued that in Seattle the local judicatory executives met together once a month. It was not an in-depth "study" session, but it had become a meeting of old friends to share experiences and let down their hair (as much as their denominational background would let them!). I was in Seattle for some contract or other, and one of the execs, perhaps the Episcopal bishop, invited me to their breakfast meeting.

Since I was the "outsider," I was politely invited to start the meeting with observations from "back East." I responded a bit, but then pointed out that I was interested in their group and in what they had found troubling in working with the congregations for which they were responsible. The LCA bishop jumped right in: "Let me tell you about my congregation in Gold Bar.[3] I've been here four years and we've had four crises in that darned place. One time, a board fight led two members to quit. One time the budget blew up midyear and I had to bail them out. Then the pastor got depressed and had to take early retirement. I forget the other crisis. But every year—trouble."

I started to talk about his data when the Methodist district superintendent interrupted: "Gold Bar? That place up the highway about fifteen miles?"

"That's it!" the Lutheran replied.

The DS continued. "I can't get anybody to stay up there. Every year the person I send to be pastor complains all year and then wants to get out ASAP."

The two of them went back and forth and then the UCC exec said, "Gold Bar? Joe, isn't that where your congregation and mine have that lawsuit going over the alley between their buildings?"

Joe, the presbytery exec, said, "Yeah. Now that you mention it. They seem to want to go to court about everything up there. Last time it had something to do with ordaining homosexuals down in Pittsburgh!"

Overwhelmed, I think I said something like, "What the hell is going on in Gold Bar?"

That started the conversation. They *all* knew something, but nobody seemed to know how to make sense of it. None of them had realized the trouble the others were experiencing. The talk went on and other things that were going on in that little town came up. I think it was the Baptist area minister who may have cracked the code. "You know. The mill closed four years ago. The sawmill. It was the only source of many jobs, but it got bought up and closed. We've all got a lot of people without jobs. Could that have anything to do with it?" My hunch is that conversation between those executives was very important in helping each of them and each of those congregations move toward what they needed to become. I just wish church executives around the country could meet each other outside their silos and have conversations like that.

We never settled that issue for Gold Bar, or wherever it actually was, but I think you can see what I mean about siloing. There was something going on in Gold Bar that was bigger than any one of the congregations—but the symptoms of whatever was bugging everybody manifested themselves in the different congregations. Yes, theologically, the church is in the world—but, in fact, if these hints are right, the world gets into the churches too. The fact that these church executives all had a different experience of the community made it possible, to some extent, to break down the individual silos of each congregation to try to understand a larger reality.

An important part of understanding and working with any congregation is sensing the world that that congregation inhabits. The temptation is to make each congregation a silo unto itself, separating its reality from all that surrounds it and its people.

As John Donne put it, "No man is an island." No congregation is an island. No denomination is an island.

"Conspirancies of Silence"

There were three congregational behaviors that seemed to be places in which there was an attempt to maintain a conspiracy of silence: conflict, sexual misconduct, and money. These were not exactly silos as we have described areas where behavior seemed to be blindered, but areas of collusion with the purpose of avoiding unsettling realities.

Early in our work in Project Test Pattern, we began to see the trauma that conflict could inflict in congregations. I ran into a remarkable clergyperson of the United Church of Christ who had just finished writing a book with Paul Kittlaus, another UCC minister, with the intimidating title: *Church Fights.*[4]

He was Speed Leas, whose work had begun in congregations in Los Angeles where all sorts of fights were occurring in congregations amid the social and racial turmoil of the late 1960s. Speed's insights were rapidly incorporated into Alban's work with congregations, and he soon joined our staff, consulting with congregations and judicatories as they struggled with their fights and training others to do so as well.

Until then, churches mostly dealt with conflict with denial. Nobody talked about it or admitted it happened. Executives and bishops did what they could to squelch the fights they knew about, and congregations were left to tear each other apart or suffer silently as supposedly wise men negotiated some sort of closure or beheading, depending on what they could figure out. Clergy or lay leaders would suddenly disappear and nobody would know what had happened or why. A pretense of peace would follow.

We could see this happening all around, although nobody talked about it. Working with pastoral change and interim ministry, we had already discovered how often congregations and pastors were victimized by lack of knowledge, uncertainty about processes, and an inability to find healing in toxic situations. Bishops and executives did what they could, but had no blueprints, or even clues, of what to do. Or even what to negotiate for!

Speed, other Alban consultants, and a growing coterie of their colleagues (many trained by Speed and using his approaches) began making a different way possible. Clergy and lay leaders were trained in conflict management *before* conflict broke out. Speed's articles and monographs, and especially his stages of conflict, gave insight and direction to those working with conflict.[5] The consultants who went through his conflict skills training helped denominational networks and continuing education centers broaden their offerings to include conflict management.

Because Alban worked across the usual denominational and regional boundaries, it was able to detect another area of denial, another conspiracy of silence. In the 1970s and 1980s issues of clergy sexual misbehavior came out of the closet. Although this had been going on for years between male clergy and female parishioners, it had always been dealt with quietly—and inadequately. The institutional church's poor response to what had often been predatory practices forced church systems to learn more and to adapt supervisory practices to the new reality, often against power systems that were not sensitive to the hidden terrible personal violations and costs. Alban was one of the first to train church executives about sexual misconduct through its Leadership Institute for Bishops and Executives, the only training at the time for denominational leaders. Nancy Hopkins and her husband, Episcopal Bishop Harold Hopkins, led Alban's training.

The issue of money surrounded the Alban Institute throughout its life. Institutionally, money was an everyday crisis for all the years

Alban existed. That is a given of this story. But a larger issue gradually emerged for us.

Because our work spanned denominations, areas, and kinds of communities, we were able to see that a gradual shrinkage of resources was going on. It wasn't just a local problem; it was everywhere. National programs were reduced. Staffs were cut back. When someone retired, they were not replaced. Everyone talked about "reorganization" and "restructuring." I noticed that none of the reorganizations or restructurings featured increased budgets; all claimed greater efficiency but none gave data about those increases of efficiency. Everything on the edge (institutions, mission congregations, experimental projects, new efforts) seemed to shrink from year to year.

The reductions were not always clear: trust funds took on new tasks, pension funds began funding clergy wellness projects or continuing education programs, agencies amalgamated. Even ordinary budgets did not go down as fast as membership did; apparently the members who stayed gave more. I tried to document some of this in what I thought was one of my more important books: *Financial Meltdown in the Mainline?*[6] As far as I could tell, the response from the churches was an uncomfortable silence.

I remember the time I was talking to an Episcopal bishop after visiting a number of his congregations and being a bit unsettled by the poor condition of some of the buildings I had seen. "Bishop," I asked, "How much deferred maintenance do you think you have in the diocese?" His reply seemed very genuine and also very sad: "I don't know," he said, "and I don't want to know."

What's Wrong with Silos

I have complained about how much trouble we make when we silo issues. That is, in one place or with one kind of people, a problem (or opportunity) arises that people try to deal with in that place or with that particular group of people. The difficulty is that the problem or difficulty is not really isolated to that place or those people, so any attempt they make to solve the problem is likely to misfire: Their effort only deals with the local manifestation of a problem that may be much broader.

A congregation gets upset because it has lost members, and it breaks its back with membership campaigns, public relations efforts, or even educational programs focused on its location and people. But the problem is bigger and more complex than the local manifestation. We found out, for example, that the membership decline some denominations in New England had identified, and were trying to fix through local efforts, was actually something going on all over New England. The focus of problem solving was siloed: each congregation working on it as if it only existed in that congregation. That just wasn't true. Each congregation needs to face its own share of the problem—revise its budget, seek outside income, or whatever can be done in their locality—but in fact somebody needs to look at the larger issue outside their silo, and develop strategies with others who are also affected by whatever is happening in New England (or in the Mainline churches, or in the culture) about people leaving churches.

At Alban we often found one set of silos that were set up as early as the sixteenth century—and in every century since. We call these silos "denominations." In the old days, in England, where my Episcopal silo was first set up, we talked about the silos first as "Church" and "dissenter," or "Anglican" and "Reformed," or "Royalist" and "evangelical." Those names changed and others were added: "Presbyterian," "Baptist," "Quaker," and, eventually, "Methodist." Each name identified part of what makes that silo special, either to its adherents or to its adversaries. The silos multiplied, but each silo saw itself as different. Sometimes our egos led us to consider our silo right, and others wrong.

It was like choosing sides, with each side being characterized by something—some points of doctrine, some issues of behavior, some religious or moral practices. Each community of people was seemingly fenced in by its emphasis, or maybe the fence was more like barbed wire, with the "right" people kept inside and the "wrong" kept out.

Few people or groups saw what Alban did, working as it did across the silos. Few people in the silos realized that many of the problems they encountered really were similar to those that troubled those in other silos. People all over New England realized that membership was sliding downward catastrophically, but they were deeply worried only about how that was affecting those in their own silo. Maryanne Rhebergen was able to see—because of a Synod-wide study—that Presbyterian membership was sliding across New England. Her silo there was New England Presbyterianism. Because I happened to be working with her on another issue, while simultaneously working in

Congregational and Methodist and Episcopal silos, I was able to see that the issue was larger even than any one denomination. Hartford Seminary's researchers, looking across the silos of church life in the Connecticut River Valley, were able to find as fact what had just been a hunch between Marianne and me.

When we talk to each other, and share with each other, we will learn more than we do when we keep our vision only within our own silo. This is a somethng that is still being learned.

CHAPTER 17

Organizing the Work: The Alban Institute's Guiding Images

In some ways, the nature of the Alban Institute depended on one's relationship with it. For some, it was a provider of helpful publications, for others a think tank, for still others a remarkable collection of consultants. Some saw it as a research organization, and others saw it as a way to keep up with what was going on in the world of congregations. It was many things to many people.

A "Linking Agency"

The first image we used was that of a "linking agency." Alban would connect congregations with those who generated knowledge they needed. We found early that there were, indeed, many groups and even institutions that had a stake in helping congregations be healthy. But we also discovered that most of the congregations needing help had difficulty locating the most helpful sources of help, and, even if they found them, knowing how to get the help they needed. Even more troublesome, many of the congregations either did not know what they needed or were allergic to asking for help. That is to say nothing of those who thought it was a sign of a failure of faith to admit they needed help.

In such a system, it was difficult for a healthy connection to be made between those needing help and those having help available.

Early in the life of the institute, we focused on that reality. In our first publication, *From Information to Action,* James Anderson and Dale Lake explored this quandary.[1] We began seeing ourselves not necessarily as generators of such help or helpful information as transmitters of it.

Our previous existence had tested the use of consultants with parishes and had taught us that knowledge and ability does not flow easily from a knowledge source to a user. Rather, the process depends heavily upon the relationship of the one to the other. In the denominational systems several enormous blockages kept helpers separated from those who needed help. We found that writing a contract between the parties was helpful in improving the relationship.

Congregations frequently did not respect or trust the purveyors of help. Local congregations often had experiences where the "higher ups" who were looked to for help were ignorant of what they really needed. Often, these "helpers" were not interested in what the congregation needed; they wanted to get the congregations involved in judicatory concerns. Communications in church systems were almost always top-down and tended to be dismissive of local concerns. In many cases, those in the help-giving locations were either uncommunicative or somewhere between unskilled and incompetent.

Right away, we discovered that thinking of ourselves as a linking agency had a built-in limitation. Who, indeed, is the "needer" of help and who is the "provider"? People tended to bring hierarchical presuppositions along with them: The people at the "top" were the providers (the judicatories, the executives, the staff people, the seminary professors or teachers, etc.) and the congregations were those who needed help.

In reality, we found, the situation was upside-down. It was the bishop who needed to know what the congregation needed, and we had to set up structures that made that backward flow of knowledge work. Both the users and the providers had important data that needed to flow to the other side, and two-way conversation was needed. The consulting relationship helped that flow happen in many cases, whatever hierarchical upset it may have caused.

The concept of a "linking agency" continued to be illuminating to us, helping us recognize that we did not always have to generate the knowledge—it often already existed in the system. In many cases our work was to help strengthen the flow of information in both directions, recognizing each as both generators of knowledge as well as users of it.

It was no accident that when we did initiate publishing as a central function of the institute, the regular publication members received from Alban had the title *Action Information*. It was *not* intended just to distribute information, but to put in people's hands information that could support them in action.

A "Think Tank"

Others called Alban a "think tank" more than we did. We welcomed what it meant, and we recognized ourselves in what they said.

We tried to be a place where thoughtful people could gather and struggle with new ideas, sometimes before the ideas were even perfected or organized very well. All through the life of the institute we were on the lookout for innovators, for imaginative people, for new ways of doing things, even new ways of understanding very old things.

Sometimes we brought people together to struggle with new ideas. Several of us discovered the remarkable work being done in England through the Grubb Institute of London, building on the psychological studies of W. R. Bion and the Tavistock Institute. Their work approached issues of dependence in ways American thinkers had not tried out. Early in Alban's life we invited Bruce Reed, the head of Grubb, to Washington, gathered a great group of American religious leaders, and spent a mind-blowing week together at the College of Preachers. In this case we went further, eventually cosponsoring with Grubb, the Tavistock Institute, Yale University, and Fordham University several ten-day conferences on group relations.[2]

We discovered that a number of remarkable clergy had found Rabbi Ed Friedman in workshops, training courses, or in a colleague group. Friedman's frame of reference was enormously useful, and we worked to get attention for his work and the associated work of Murray Bowen in the family systems. We helped publicize and distribute Friedman's book, *Generation to Generation*.[3]

As noted earlier, we found the pioneering work Speed Leas and Paul Kittlaus had done in conflict management on the West Coast and brought the wisdom of conflict management to congregations.

Sometimes we simply acted as scouts, locating information and making it available to religious constituencies who otherwise might not know about it. In many cases that meant things like bringing exciting research already done by, say, Presbyterians in California to others who had never heard of it in other parts of the country. To be truthful, we also found that often people in the *same* denomination— or even the same judicatory—as those who did the research had never heard of it, either. This was a result of the siloing characteristic in the churches, and it was something we could help overcome.

A local pastor in New York State who followed the work of Alban attended a conference at which Russell Ackoff of Wharton School in Philadelphia gave a remarkable talk on what "systems" really are. Alban took the cassette on which the pastor recorded the talk, contracted with Dr. Ackoff, and made it available as a monograph.[4]

Carl Dudley's remarkable paper on rural congregations became another Alban Institute monograph, *The Unique Dynamics of the Small Congregation,* in 1977.

When Bruce Reed's landmark book (see note 66 above) came out, we contracted with Urban T. Holmes, a budding pastoral theologian of note, to review it in *Action Information*. Later, Reed gave us a great paper, *The Task of the Church and the Role of Its Members.*

Action Information itself, beginning in 1975 with four issues each year, eventually expanding to six issues, became a regular way to broadcast the practical knowledge the Alban staff and our contacts shared with each other. There, under the stewardship of Celia Hahn, the pioneering work of the institute in working with practical knowledge was carried out.

A Departmental Organization

It is probably clear by now that the Alban Institute was a floating crap game. It started with high hopes and ran straight into a survival crisis. It never outgrew either its high hopes or its survival crisis.

But with its ground-level commitment to strengthening the life of the local religious congregation, it took on tasks and challenges as they arose. As time went on, we began to sort out what we could do into several groups of activities. Perhaps the longest-lived of the images we used was one of an organization with several functioning departments: (1) publications; (2) consulting; (3) research; (4) education; and (5) development.[5]

Publications was the department at the heart of what we were. Led by Celia Hahn, Alban Publications quickly made a name for the institute, distributing our learnings widely in the religious world. We expanded slowly in this area, trying at first to get established publishers to put out things we knew were important to congregation leaders. Many of these publications were small, so commercial publishers were reluctant to get involved. When Jack Harris's book *Stress, Power, and Ministry* came along, we knew parish clergy and leaders needed to know about what Jack described. We failed to find a publisher to take it on, so we expanded into the publication of small books. It became our first real publishing success.

To see Alban's lasting influence in churches, one need only look at any bookstore's shelves or catalogues to see the remarkable wealth of books that are practical, direct, and inexpensive that other publishers now make available to those who need them. Few such books were available before Alban began publishing them.

Consulting is a complicated field, and "consulting" is used in many conflicting ways. We decided early on that we were not called to be *experts* in specific fields (like finance, or demographics, or theology). We were experts at what the professionals call "process consultation." Basically, that meant that we helped people understand what it was that was giving them trouble and help them develop structures to work on that trouble. We would work with teams to learn how to approach the trouble and, when possible, solve it. We helped people find and use various kinds of expertise when it was needed.

Here's an example of process consultation at work. I once was asked to help a United Methodist Conference staff decide how to divvy up the available congregations into workable clusters so they could appoint pastors more effectively. I did not know beans about how they made such decisions, so I was very reluctant to get involved. But I asked them who was on the committee to work on the problem. They named the nine people on the committee: Three had multiple years' experience as district superintendents, making such decisions annually; one was the bishop, who had been a district superintendent for six years; four were senior clergy with many years of pastoral experience; and the other was the conference executive. Every one of them had been through the pastoral appointment system at least five times. Well, you may be surprised, but I took the job and did it pretty well. Why? Not because I knew what I was doing. Not because I was an expert in Methodism or understood the conference as well or better than anybody there, because I didn't pass muster on *any* of those criteria. I did the job well because I knew that the expertise, experience, and wisdom of that whole conference was already there. I knew how to dig that knowledge out of them. I knew how to help them listen to each other. I knew I could help them make good decisions, and I knew I could help them work out differences they might have. They already had the smarts; I knew how to help them get access to their own wisdom and focus it so they could do what they needed to do.

Our consultants were *not* klutzes. Some developed enormous expertise in a number of areas (like Speed Leas on conflict management and organizational structure, Roy Oswald on clergy stress and congregational anxiety, and Ed White on denominational dynamics). But what they could do, like few others I've known, was hear what was going on, see the tight spots, and steer the group from chaos to focus.[6]

We already knew that the process works best when consultants are paid by and responsible to the congregation, but it's not always that simple. Sometimes the congregation needs help paying and the judicatory has to get involved. If necessary, this can work, but the congregation needs to control the relationship. The critical issue is control. Judicatories are always tempted to control the congregations, which they could do if the consultant acted as judicatory staff. We believed the congregation needed to be able to fire the consultant.

Such consulting, from the beginning, was a key tool used by Alban. Another important role of the consultant at Alban was, as it had been at Project Test Pattern, as an observer, learner, and research agent, piling up knowledge that can be shared through publications and training events with others. What we learned in one place often had implications for many other congregations, judicatories, and even denominations.

A Research Agency

Alban always suffered in its image as a place that did research. It had no laboratories. It had minimal skills in statistical analysis. For a long time, it did not possess much in the way of computers. It published no learned tomes and offered no degrees. It talked about theology, but called it "operational theology." It honored information and information science, but talked about something called action information. Its published material is not often noted in professional journals.[7] It never quite fit in.

It may be that the problem was our methods—we built on the concepts Parker Palmer and Elden Jacobson articulated as "Action Research."[8] This form of research as we practiced it involved more informal protocols, but involved the formation of hypotheses, the gathering of data through methods that engaged the subjects of the research, and their mobilization to test the hypotheses. As we used the methods, a round of testing led to one of analysis, then adjustment of the hypothesis to the new situation generated by the initial intervention, and then a new intervention based on a revision of the original intervention. It was messy. Not clean. It engaged the subjects of the research in the whole enterprise, and the end product expected was a changed situation, not simply the articulation of information. In essence, it was a combination of conventional research thinking with some of the elements of organizational development.

The work I have already described on the pastoral start-up and interim ministry followed this pattern. The result was some significant learning about a dynamic period in congregational life, but also the invention of a new role in pastoral leadership, a new training program for interim pastors, and even a national network for interim pastor support. One piece led to another. And each iteration of the research produced not only knowledge (some of it in written material) but also a population of people committed to changed behaviors.

Specific projects tended to leak into related issues, produce new research spinoffs, or generate new areas of activity. For example, our work on parish consultation in Project Test Pattern led us to new research on the change of pastors. That led to the interim pastor work and, as I have described, into the study of congregations with endowments. It also led us to work on the issue of clergy sabbaticals and other long periods of clergy absence, and to the phenomenon of the long-tenured pastor.

Few were stand-alone activities. We understood we were not aiming our work simply at new knowledge—we wanted to affect the future of congregations. Meanwhile, we were constrained to work only on efforts that generated sufficient funding to pay for the activity.

In 1976 Alban received three competitive research grants from the Lilly Endowment. One was actually a spin-off of our work on pastoral start-up. A Presbyterian colleague had asked us to investigate the "first start-up"—the time when a prospective seminary graduate is assigned to his or her first assignment. He and others had seen many seminary graduates "crash and burn" in their first parish, and they wondered whether we could understand that time better and see what could be done.

The Boundary Project

We called it the Boundary Project. It was characteristic of our more focused efforts at research, and it had a lot of payoff not only in what we learned, but also in organizational change in a number of theological seminaries.

This started in an interesting dialogue with the granter. The Lilly Endowment notified us that they wanted to initiate work on six areas in which they thought we might be interested—and we were. Eventually we sent proposals in three of the areas they named, one of which was the question of how to help seminary graduates make a more constructive entry into their first congregational assignment.

It was clear that Alban's interest in the First Start-up and the endowment's interest in improving the effectiveness of the seminary graduate in first assignments were about the same thing. But as I pondered what we already knew, I saw a flaw in what the foundation was asking for. At that point in time, seminaries around the country had made many efforts to try to do just what the endowment wanted to help them do:

- For nearly a century, seminaries had been inventing and putting to use the disciplines of pastoral care. They had new courses, even new departments, broadening their faculties in practical areas;
- Seminaries had stimulated the development of pastoral theology and brought in new scholars, many trained in the new disciplines;
- Seminaries had changed courses to emphasize sociological understandings to go along with historical studies;
- Seminaries had invented a variety of kinds of fieldwork to give parish experience to students and had experimented with ways to supervise those students;

- Seminaries had even experimented with year-long internships of students in specially prepared congregations;
- Seminaries had welcomed the insights of psychological study and many of the behavioral sciences to their courses;
- Seminaries had welcomed clinical pastoral education to the world of theological education, giving course credit for such work.

Frankly, we thought, what else can they do?

What hit us immediately was the realization that the issue was not the seminaries, and it could not be fixed in the seminaries. The problem was, rather, in the transition from the seminary to the congregation. Seminaries were doing all they could. The problem was not in the seminary *or* in the congregation; it was somehow in the transition from one to the other.

We realized the problem was at the boundary between seminary and congregation. It could not be solved in either seminary or congregations because the problem was in the transition. We wrote that into our proposal, and the foundation responded by allocating funds to help us study it.

At that point, Roy Oswald joined the institute full-time to lead the study. Since we already had the funds to do it, we didn't need to rely on our tried-and-true Tom Sawyer method, so we decided to pull out another method with which we'd had success—we decided to "Kübler-Ross" the issue by going to the people living in the problem and asking them about it.[9] We would study what happened as seminary graduates actually crossed the boundary between life in seminary and their work in the their first congregation.

And that is what Roy did. He built contracts with ten theological centers to join in the study. In each place he formed teams *with* the faculties of the seminaries and carried out several activities:

- The faculty agreed to list the areas in which they wanted their graduates to be knowledgeable and competent, using the seminary's or the denomination's list of vital competencies.
- The faculty agreed to name a dozen to two dozen of their graduates of the last year or two whose judgment they valued.
- Those graduates were invited to a two-to-three-day seminar at the seminary, at which time the joint team of Alban consultant and seminary faculty engaged the graduates to evaluate how well the graduates felt their seminary education had equipped them while

they were in seminary in the areas the seminary and the denomination agreed were vital. The graduates also evaluated how well they could operate in their congregational placement in those same areas.

- After the evaluations, the graduates and the faculty members engaged in dialogue about making future transitions more constructive.

- For each seminary, Roy Oswald prepared a report of the findings for the seminary faculty.

The institute published a monograph by Roy Oswald, *Crossing the Boundary,* that was used by many seminaries, judicatories, and by hundreds of seminary graduates to get perspective on their own transition issues. Quite a few seminaries—Columbia Theological Seminary in Decatur, Georgia, was the first we were aware of—have made major adjustments to how graduates are "launched" and supported through the early years of the first appointment.

We had, and still have, two concerns about how this all worked out. We had two hopes for our work: (1) We wanted seminaries to have regular ways to get feedback from their graduates so they could revise their teaching, and (2) we wanted seminaries to help graduates establish regular patterns of post-graduation education and growth. Neither of these hopes was achieved, although the knowledge from the project did get wide distribution and many post-seminary projects were later launched across the country.[10]

We also discovered the uncomfortable way that religious groups oversimplify the acquisition of knowledge. In too many cases, seminaries bought the monograph about what Roy had discovered in those ten seminaries and simply passed on information to their graduates about other people in other settings rather than doing research on their own experience.

We learned a lot about crossing the boundary, and we shared what we had learned, but there were no takers on building in continuing research and dialogue between faculties and graduates after graduation.

Congregational Growth and the Inviting Church

Many congregations throughout the country experienced membership losses after the roaring fifties of almost universal church growth. The curves of membership were mixed: Nondenominational evangelical congregations were stronger in gains longer than the denominational "Mainline." Mainline declines were earlier and more threatening, especially in New England. The most important work Alban did on this issue may have been the New England study with Hartford Seminary, which recognized the cross-denominational, cross-jurisdictional nature of the losses. It was the first signal to local congregations and their judicatories that the problem was more than local, and that their silos were blinding them to the regional, if not national, nature of the problem.

Alban spent some time analyzing what was going on, studying the situation as we worked in various places, and produced some resources on the situation and what to do about it. Breaking down the elements of bringing new members into congregations, which is the place to start when looking for growth in the number of members, we identified several issues to which we needed to pay attention.

Our first question was, "Why does someone who is not a church member decide to go to church?" Why do they want to "try it out" and show up at a congregation one Sunday morning? A lot of techniques about how to trigger such behavior in nonchurch members had been taught to church members for a while, but there was little confidence that the methods of the nineteenth century would still work. Some of the techniques, such as revivals and evangelism campaigns, actually seemed to turn people off, and worked mostly to increase the commitment of the people who were already members.

We also recognized how some membership-growth techniques tempted church members to use psychological coercion on others. If, indeed, a member's own commitment to God depended on convincing others to join the church, people would go to great lengths to sign up others. For those in less committed or outgoing traditions, there was something slightly uncomfortable and self-serving about talking somebody else into joining your church.

In the end, what we did know was that every week people who were not members of that or any other church just showed up. Nobody knew why; it just happened. And most churches recognized the phenomenon and wondered how they could help those visitors become dedicated, committed new members of the congregations.

So our next question was, "What can move a *visitor* to a *potential member* and then to a *committed member*?" Using funds from several small grants, supplemented by fees for services, we turned Roy Oswald and Speed Leas loose to explore the early stages of church membership of people who "just showed up."

The two of them did extensive work with a group of congregations—many in the Indianapolis area—interviewing people who joined new-member classes. The results were eye opening, as we had expected. We had often found that people who are new to a system see things the old-time members simply don't see. We first focused on what the new members had found that made it difficult for them to find their way into the congregation. These were often simple things, such as "They couldn't locate the doors" or "The announcement said to meet in the narthex" (whatever the hell that was!). Roy and Speed collaborated on a book that described what they found: *The Inviting Church: A Study of New Member Assimilation,* published by Alban in 1987.

Many congregations learned to look out for the things we had found in those Indianapolis congregations, and in many cases built better member-entry processes. To our disappointment, very few congregations went further; we had hoped they would begin using similar research to discover how their member-entry process was not working well. They learned from what we had learned in Indianapolis, but few began a regular process of checking out how to improve their own processes of welcoming the people who "just showed up."

A second part of the work Roy and Speed did was to ask those same people what it was that helped them make the transition into membership. Again, many found ideas that helped bring members in, but few went deeper to turn their attention and research to how they themselves were already doing well in welcoming.

Unfinished, because unfunded, was further research we wanted to do with the people who "just showed up" but then decided not to become members. We believe those people had information congregations need very much. Most congregations, we found, lost those names before long, also losing what those people could have told them. Speed and Roy led many congregational workshops on the subject of the Inviting Church, and other researchers joined in spreading this practical knowledge widely in the churches. Few congregations that we know of, however, have continued to be learning congregations, interviewing their own members for up-to-date knowledge.

Another piece of work Alban did was to translate the work of the Anglican Church of New Zealand. Work done there under the

archdeacon of Auckland, Ted Buckle, studied the suburban congregations established after World War II, and discovered that our
language about church growth is too limited. My book *More Than
Numbers* brings Buckle's work and insights from New Zealand to the
American scene.[11]

Buckle's insight, and my translation of it, suggests that our
churches are too tightly focused on enlarging the membership of the
congregation as the only definition of what "church growth" means.
True church growth involves at least four distinct areas or types of
growth.[12]

- Numerical Growth: This is growth in the ways we ordinarily
  describe it, including Sunday attendance, size of budget, and
  number of activities, all based on having more members and more
  active members.
- Maturational Growth: This is growth in the faith and maturity of
  each member and member's ability to nurture and be nurtured;
- Organic Growth: This is growth of the congregation as a functioning community, able to maintain itself as a living organism and
  as an institution that can engage the other institutions of society;
- Incarnational Growth: This is growth in the ability to take the
  meanings and values of the faith-story and make them real in
  the world and society outside the congregation. The congregation
  grows in its ability to enflesh in the community what the faith is
  all about.

Two key elements make up this alternative view to church growth:

- The numerical growth that everybody worries about is not the
  only way that congregations can and do grow. Indeed, many congregations probably—for demographic or other reasons—may never
  be successful in numerical growth. However, any congregation,
  numerically growing or not, has the possibility of achieving significant growth in other, possibly equally important ways.
- There are practical approaches and simple and usable activities and
  processes through which any congregation's leaders can work on
  any of the four kinds of growth. Indeed, failure at any one of the
  kinds of growth may best be dealt with by switching the *kind* of
  growth the congregation is attempting to achieve.

Over the years Alban not only used the ideas and methods Parker Palmer and Elden Jacobson proposed as Action Research; we tried, with little success, to encourage groups and congregations to do such research themselves. There is no problem or opportunity an individual congregation cannot face if they would adopt an open approach to research by studying their situation, trying new things, and seeing what happens. Then trying again.[13]

An Educational Institution

We honestly thought everything we did was educational. In time, as Alban grew and broadened the areas in which it worked, it came to organize education as a department of the institute, although our staff operated across the departments.

Indeed, we understood our work of consulting truly as education. Perhaps the most useful education, since the clients of the consultation engaged directly with the consultant to explore the issue and jointly plan ways to address it. Education happened in the middle of it all, with client and consultant becoming a learning team.

Education as one of Alban's formal efforts grew out of our consulting. As consultants and congregations or judicatories worked on defining and solving problems, new knowledge emerged, and the consultants were called on both to do formal teaching and to engage in more relationships in which educational consultation occurred.

Certain specialties grew out of the work we did. Roy Oswald got called on to work with issues of clergy role, function, and leadership. He explored those issues with clergy and he did research with them, using the literature of the behavioral sciences. The culmination of that work was the remarkable Clergy Development Institute, a ten-day engagement two or three times a year with a fascinating cadre of clergy willing to face the challenge of personal and professional growth

Speed Leas developed a Consultant Training Course that produced scores of the crisis consultants that were called on all across the churches whenever a "church fight" broke out. And they broke out often. Both he and Roy were called on to help clergy, executives, and others get on board with new research. With the help of a grant from the Hewlett Foundation, Speed was able to enlarge our resources in conflict management by adding Roy Pneuman, Margaret Bruell, and George Parsons as consultants.

For ten years, Alban had an annual ten-day Leadership Institute for Bishops and Executives, those charged with regional oversight of congregations. When we realized that much denominational education for these executive leaders was only orienting the new leaders to programs the denomination needed them to manage, not recognizing that new knowledge and new problems were invading their territory, our institute worked at training them in the processes they would need to do their job well. Most new executives had little experience in that kind of leadership role, having mostly served previously as pastors. Many had little experience supervising clergy before their selection or election as bishop, general presbyter, president of the conference, or district superintendent. In the early years we brought in specialists in emerging issues: Rabbi Ed Friedman with resources in family systems and Harold and Nancy Hopkins with resources in sexual boundary issues. An important byproduct of those events, of course, was the linkages that were forged between leaders of different denominations.

Infrastructure Miscalculations

At Alban, from the beginning, we underestimated the importance of our own infrastructure. The level of management and financing to do the work we took on—to mount research efforts and projects, to develop wide-ranging educational programs, to publish excellent publications, to deploy first-class, multitalented consultants, to train people and oversee work in multiple situations and locations—were too often neglected.

Our attention was on the difficulties of church bodies—especially congregations—not on how we as an organization held our corporate existence together. Our focus was on developing resources, solving problems, and delivering help to others. That was and remained our true Plan A. We thought that carrying out that plan would provide adequate financial and organizational resources to support us enough to carry on.

When the support we had counted on for our original Plan A did not materialize—when it became obvious that we would not have foundation support—we settled for a group of miscellaneous fundraising activities, hoping they would undergird our work. Almost miraculously that grab-bag system gradually grew to the level of keeping us alive—never secure, but at least alive—long enough to produce a remarkable set of resources.

We had no real strategy, just tactics. Elements of our support system grew to include the following: (1) Fees for consulting services: My personal goal was to generate enough to provide 133 percent of the costs of my office; the goal of each consultant was to cover the costs for the consultant plus an "overage" to cover some of the institute's costs. (2) Income from publications: Whatever came in over costs of doing business plus royalties. Royalties for my publications went to the institute, but all other publications paid royalties to the authors. (3) Income from memberships in the institute. (4) A few small foundation grants for specific projects or activities. Trinity Church, New York, for example, made a grant to help support the publications program. (5) Occasional windfall grants and gifts like the one for $7,500 from Mac Wilson that saved us at our founding. There were no subsidies from denominations or congregations, other than occasional gifts, many from pastors' "discretionary funds."

In the early years we did what we could to cover costs. Very early, I could patch up weak places simply by taking on more contracts for the fees they generated. We cut costs more than we should have. I had always wanted income from consulting to cover the costs of regular meetings of the consultants and a director to oversee and strengthen their work. We never reached that level, although for a short time we had Terry Foland fill that role on a part-time basis. We limited the meetings of the consultants, making it harder for them to exchange knowledge and skills. Such meetings were expensive in themselves, but they also pulled the consultants out of fee-generating work. Similar difficulty made it impossible to have someone oversee research projects. As executive director of the institute, I did what I could to oversee consultants and research work. This constant battle to cover costs also held salaries below what these skilled people could make as independent workers, so we lost several of them to higher-paying secular work.

In order to support the urgent needs of congregations, we stretched ourselves more than we probably should have, and we underfunded our need for a supportive infrastructure. We were not the first or last organization to tell this story, but we had, by finding ways to

support ourselves, lasted longer than many others that might have
had more promising beginnings.

Moving On

It became time for me to leave Alban. I loved what we were doing in
the crazy world of institutional religion, but I didn't enjoy running
an organization that had to battle for every inch of progress. One
that did not fit expectations, that insisted on pursuing issues others
wanted to ignore (none of the denominations, for example, were
willing to admit that "firing clergy" actually happened or needed to
be looked at). I left to become a freelance church meddler.

But how to do that? How does the founder of an organization leave it so that it can continue its work—we had few examples
of founders leaving such an organization without its usually immediate collapse. We had learned that most organizations went belly-up
when the founder left—and we could only find one book about how
founders left even secular organizations. Apparently it isn't easy.

We had learned that organizations could be helped by having a
skillful outsider come in to consult at crucial moments of life. So
Alban hired consultants to help. Art Frentzrab, a local development
consultant who had helped invent capital campaigns for universities, came in to help strengthen our board and build up our capital
resources. Vance and Mary Johnson, organization consultants experienced in institutional change, came in to help shape organization
expectations and advise me on my responsibilities in leaving. Bart
Lloyd worked with me on my personal job shift.

It became clear that my work needed to move toward articu-
lating as clearly as possible what we had been doing and what we had
learned in that effort. Although the Johnsons insisted on my "stating
our vision" in a twenty-five-word statement, I blew the assignment
entirely.

I wrote a book instead. *The Once and Future Church* described the
paradigmatic change that churches were experiencing and how this
change was shifting all the roles and relationships within religious life
in the Christian world our churches inhabited. I proposed a three-age
timeline for Christianity: First was the age of the "apostolic church,"
then the much-longer "age of Christendom" whose disintegration we

were currently living through, and then the "emerging age" we were anticipating.[14]

The book came out in 1991 as Alban and I began preparing for my leaving. It hit a popular nerve in the churches and became a best seller. It also kicked me into further writing: *Transforming Congregations for the Future* and *Five Challenges for the Once and Future Church*.[15] All tried to share learnings from the Alban years.

Two other books came out of research I had begun while at Alban. One, *More Than Numbers*, was mentioned earlier in this book in the discussion of church growth. The other, *Financial Meltdown in the Mainline*, was on an issue that grew larger for me in the period after Alban but was sparked while at Alban.

All of these books came out of my reflection on the work we did and were doing at Alban, and all speak about the nature of religious institutional life as it was lived in the Western part of Christendom.

CHAPTER 18

Operational Theology: A Reprise

Throughout this book I have been focused on a developing story of a particular ministry, a story that has personal implications because it is the story of my work with colleagues within the institutional structures of what we have come to call Protestant Mainline churches of the United States.[1]

We learned more than I know how to talk about, but it never fit into the formal categories of theology—neither "systematic" nor "biblical"; not even "historical" nor "practical." Early on I realized we were dealing with something different, and I tried to call it "operational theology." I saw the specialists in academic theologies as "pure scientists," like chemists or physicists; I characterized our more practical work of operational theology as "engineering."

I want to share a few anecdotes pointing to this category of knowledge, with the intent of highlighting what I think is one of the key reasons why I insist that the life of local congregations is, indeed, the locus of very important even if unarticulated theological content.

It was my first pastorate. I was young, probably twenty-five, and had been priest in charge for just a couple of months. I had been there long enough to have become thoroughly intimidated by the presence of one of my laymen, I'll call him Alexander Allison (everybody called him Alex). He was smart. He seemed to know how to negotiate small town life with more savoir-faire than I'd ever seen. He was a prominent businessman. In everything I could think of, he had more of what people needed to have than I had hopes of ever having. The problem facing me, his pastor, was that all of a sudden his mother had

died. I had gotten to know her slightly in my frantic parish calling
two months earlier when I had arrived in the town, but really did not
know him or the family in any depth.

I knew it was my job to go see Alex. When somebody's parent dies,
the pastor goes to call. *Everybody* knows that. But every bone in my
body was scared, intimidated, unsure. I couldn't think of anything
to say. None of what I knew about death and dying fit, I didn't think.
Shoot, I didn't know what I thought except that I didn't want to go
see Alex, but that I had to.

Honestly I didn't want to turn on the car. Putting the key in the
ignition was hard. I drove by Alex's house twice. The first time I just
flunked out and started home. The second time I stopped out front
and twiddled my thumbs for a while. Listen—I mean this and I'm still
embarrassed thinking about it half a century later—I did *not* want to
go in. But I knew I had to. Finally, I cranked myself up with a shallow
piece of bad theology—"God saw we were a mess, so he sent Jesus"—
and I repeated that to myself all the way up the walkway to the house,
and then, hesitating, I said it to myself once more to get me to push
the doorbell button. I was in a state. A funk. I hoped nobody came to
the door.

No luck. The door opened. It was Alex behind the screen door.

He threw it open and embraced me, saying, "Loren, thanks for
coming. Come on in!" I did. It tasted like grace, and it was. He may
never have known what was going on. Not many people ever knew it
before you read this.

You see, I thought it was my job to have the answer. To bring with
me the fullness of God's presence, or at least an ability to articulate
it all clearly. No way. God was fully already there, and we, those who
happened to be there that night, including Alex, received that presence freely before we even had an inkling of it.

That's the ordinary stuff of parish life: God's presence and grace
interpenetrating what's going on. It can be found in the dialogue
between people, but it's there before they call it to attention. It's the
stuff of life. Talking about it is what I call operational theology.

Another category is what I came to call "hunches." Driving
through downtown Chapel Hill I saw somebody I remembered from
the parish. Alicia was her name. She was off and on about worship.
Showed up from time to time, but she was not a regular. I didn't know
her well, and she kept up a bit of a "don't mess with me" air about her.

That afternoon I suddenly felt I ought to check in with her, so I pulled into a parking place, got out, and walked over to where she was sitting on a bench on the sidewalk. We chatted a bit, but I couldn't get much sense of where she was and in fifteen or twenty minutes I went on about my business. When I got to my office about half an hour later I got a phone call from her, wanting to have a talk. Turned out she was contemplating suicide, and we were able to get her to some helpful therapy in time. She even turned up at church a few times after that. I'd had no idea what was going on, but I had a hunch. After a few like that, I decided that hunches were something to pay attention to.

I think all this is also an indicator of the ordinary working of the energy, the power, and the presence of the One because of whom we have things like parishes, the One we worship together. Another face of operational theology.

CHAPTER 19

The Calling We All Have

What does all this mean, this long story about working with parishes across the country?[1]

The focus here has been on efforts to work with, understand, and improve the work of congregations in a number of denominations. Many of the parishes we worked with were linked together by common meanings, history, theology, or denominational connection. These linkages sometimes functioned like the silos that keep grain separated on farms, and those silos often blocked communication or separated people or groups from each other. They have, therefore, often been a problem, keeping us from seeing that others suffer from problems we also experience from collaborating with them and getting in the way of learning from each other.

Being siloed often blocks us from truths others have discovered. We can become blind to the gifts of others and overlook the gifts being nurtured in other silos. Indeed, we can become allergic to and dismissive of gifts from outside our own world. The inward orientation of our silos blocks us from knowing why others find *us* to be the problem! We lose the capacity to see ourselves as others see us, as Robert Burns put it.

But the way we silo ourselves is not entirely negative. To be in a silo with others can have healthy positive effects—it can help us clarify our own life and learn from others with similar leanings. It can protect us from cacophony, from being overwhelmed by all sorts of different voices when we are not yet sure of our own. It can help us live into the specialness of commonality within our own giftedness. It can help us clarify our own special gifts.

The Parish as Ecclesia

At the very heart of our enterprise is a simple fact. We are not a bunch of people who met at midday one day and decided to form a club. Not even a very nice club to do all sorts of good things for people.

We have been "called." We have a long history of being called. Abraham was called out of his father's land. From the beginning the call was dialogical—God calls Abraham; Abraham responds in faith. The whole people of Israel lived into the dialogue: a life of being called into relationship and then rebelling against it—a life of tragedy and triumph, a life full of God's faithfulness and the people's unfaithfulness, followed by God's redemption of them and a renewed call.

Our calling out as church and as parishes is shot through the New Testament, but I particularly like the statement in Luke when Jesus was asked to read in the synagogue in Nazareth, his home town:

> The Spirit of the Lord is upon me, because he has anointed me to bring good news to the poor. He has sent me to proclaim release to the captives and recovery of sight to the blind, to let the oppressed go free, to proclaim the year of the Lord's favor.[2]

This part of his calling us out is the backside of what he calls the "good news," and it articulates the character of what we are called out for. The good news he announces is itself in dialogical form—he tells us first the bad news we are called to proclaim and then, I would argue, the good news we are called to act out. The bad news for the prisoner is prison; the good news is release from captivity. Bad news for the blind is blindness; the good news is to be able to see. Bad news for broken victims is brokenness and victimhood; good news is to be set free.

Simple, right? But this is not a list of three or four things the church is to set right. It is a vivid cry to us to be at work in setting the world and ourselves right. It means that we are called to locate those things causing pain and separation and sickness and loneliness and hate—locate them wherever they exist in our world and then break our back tearing them out and banishing them.

Yes, it calls us out, but it does so in the service of the good news he is here to proclaim. His kingdom is a place where hurts are healed, where tears are wiped away, where even death itself, the greatest enemy of all, is to be done away with. That may be proclamation, but in truth it is a proclamation that the old world is no more, that the revolution of his kingdom is already present, and that it is the business of his community of faith to be at work on it. It's not a spark in the darkness, it is a blinding flash of an absolutely new light. The light that darkness cannot overcome. Ever.

Maybe, just maybe, there is a glimpse here of why we may have needed to silo as much as we have. Maybe there is a fear in us that if we don't fence this light in, if we don't put up impermeable walls around it, it might get dissipated and lost. So we protect it by trying to wall it in. Keep it safe so the wrong people won't know about it.

That's not his way. That blinding light is here to stay. That's our good news. That's not all, of course. There is the evidence of his being there to death and beyond. His refusal to back off, even if it leads to the cross. His many articulations that he claims us and loves us will never desert us, no matter what. That we are God's children and his friends.

But we, we are so different. So diverse. Living in different worlds, having different cultures, even values. Peter Berger, one of our great scholars and wise men, talks about how we all seem to want to find some ground that's certain to undergird our faith, as well as our incredulity that it's really real, that it's not a chimera of our imagination or hope. Berger tells us that some want to put their trust in our religious structures and to feel that the way we put our institutions together is faultless and reflects the "right" way to be the church. Others put their trust in absolute certainty that they have the right interpretation of our religious texts. They have no doubt, but excellent scholars differ on many large questions. Berger says that others of us have reached certainty because we just know in our hearts that it is true. We are convinced and claim our certainty there—in spite of the enormous questions psychology brings to how our emotions and minds work.

Even at the deepest levels of our faith, we tend to gather in silos.

Transformative Congregations

Parishes are a special form of human community. At the heart of every parish is a motley crowd of ordinary people, each with an individual sense of self as well as a different capacity to perceive or ignore calls from the outside. Every parish I have been part of has some people of extraordinary openness and wisdom as well as some as open and wise as a brick wall. Just as each parish is unique, each constituent member is unique. Each one got there through a formation process of family (including genetic history) and friends, rivals and enemies. Over the years, we have learned something—but not much—about these differing paths, but at best what shows up in any parish is a mysterious collection of human beings. In the course of many years and hundreds of presentations, I have used a process to help congregations understand the uniqueness of the different people who gather there and how they relate to each other.

Let me ask you to engage with me in a quick exploration of the mystery of a parish. I have two sets of questions for you. In the first set, choose a number between 1 and 10, and in the second, choose a letter between A and J. There is no trick, no right answer, just an opportunity for you to choose for right now where you are on two continua. And it is just for now; you can change in 20 minutes if you want to find another, better place on the continua. Humor me. Choose your responses to indicate where you are between the opposites in the questions.

First, on the 1 to 10 scale: How do you believe one knows God best? An answer of 1 means "I feel I know God best in a one-on-one individual, personal relationship." An answer of 10 means "I believe I know God best in the midst of God's people, the church." So between what I defined as point 1 and point 10, where would you put yourself right now? Take your time, then write the number down.

Second, on the A to J scale: What is the purpose of life? Point A represents "I believe the end of life, the purpose of life, is to have lived so that I am united with God at my death." Point J is different: "I believe that the end of life, the purpose of life, is to work with my brothers and sisters to build a world of peace, love, and justice." So, choose where you are now (remember, you can change whenever you want to—this isn't a permanent commitment on your part!) and write it down.

Then draw a graph and place yourself and others on it.

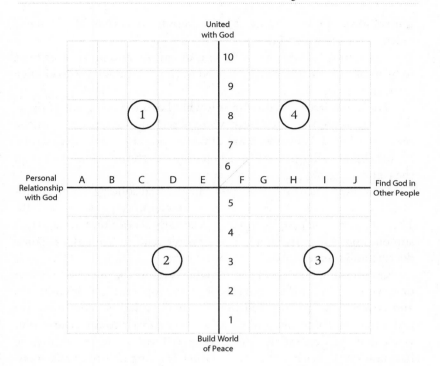

When I have done this all across the country, I have people name their coordinates (like "my location is C-8"), and I simply place an X at that spot. As the group, one by one, places themselves and see the locations, the graph always becomes a loose scattering of Xs, and the group sees visually how diverse they really are—even though EVERY possible position on the graph is well within what some people see as an "orthodox" position. A lot becomes clear as we realize that we in the church really are a rich collection of folks, and not at all defined by specific rational or theological positions.

Look at the graph. It's shape, overall, is that of a cross. The crucial dynamic of every congregation is that those Xs, representing each one of us, are not stationary, but moving, moving as if in orbit around the center of the cross. Every week, we, the dispersed Xs, are drawn back to the center of the cross, where we are renewed in the activity of worship. For me, that is the Eucharist, where we take into our lives and bodies the bread and wine of the sacrament. I have no doubt that many on the graph have other ingredients of worship that are more central for them, but for me, it is in the Eucharist that I find myself renewed for life where I live it.

The four quadrants are different, of course, and most of us tend to be in one or the other over a period of time, although we do change from time to time.

The upper left hand quadrant is what I call the quadrant of those who want to go deep with God, who are seeking an experience of the presence of God. People who are drawn to prayer groups, spirituality. People slightly allergic to those in quadrant 3, the one that's below on the right.

Quadrant 2 is people who are healers, often solitary, rarely group-oriented (the bane of people who want committees to work well). They are often the people who go to the early service on Sunday, then slip out and skip coffee hour. These people tend to work alone. Some doctors and businesspeople are found here.

Quadrant 3, down and to the right, is home for our activists, the ones who see things that aren't right, that people suffer from injustice and poverty, and get engaged to try to make it better. They organize task forces to fix things and are often very caustic toward those who won't join their crusades. They have a civil war going on with those in quadrant 1—neither thinks the other is doing anything that matters! Pastors often have trouble mollifying residents of either of these quadrants, because they are both convinced that everything would be OK if all those "stupid spiritualists" or "hopeless activists" would join them.

Quadrant 4, up and to the right, is home for some of us who just know in our bones that the state of the whole community, the congregation, the parish is important! They want to build it up, increase its membership, bring in people, make the board really work. They'll work tirelessly to make things go.

A parish with any of those quadrants empty has a hard time. Having them full does not guarantee peace and quiet, but it covers the bases. And it makes the worship rich and varied, strengthening each member with different ways of seeing things.

The work we did in PTP and Alban helped us see and influence these dynamics: In a congregation the activities related to worship have an ability to shape much about people; the dynamics between those identified as religious leaders and the ordinary members are full of energy and meaning; the sense of how traditions have reached them is deeply important but differs with different people and different generations; a sense of "the holy" may be indefinable in any detail, but has shaping power; the way God is conceived and dealt with makes all the difference; the way things are used matters deeply (things like bread and wine and water; things like places of holy memory).

We truly deal here with deep mystery, something not at all definable.

I have come to think of a parish metaphorically, rather than try to pin the mystery down.

A parish is like a large, brilliant, clear prism sitting on a table with sunlight pouring in from windows on every side. We know how prisms act in such a situation. They multiply and enrich the light and the color.

The strong light pours into the prism, which catches the light and refracts it, splitting it into all the colors of the spectrum. The stronger the light, the more spectacular the colors that come out and sparkle on the walls. What seems to be a small piece of glass generates a kaleidoscope of color.

One light, but many facets. Many colors.

So, too, for our parishes. Many quadrants, even more individuals within those quadrants. Individuals orbiting around the center, the cross; being restored and strengthened by the center.

But the light is one light. The calling we all have, the calling to belong to the One who is the light, the light of the world.

Endnotes

Preface

1. Reuel Howe, in the preface to my *New Hope for Congregations* (New York: Seabury Press), 5.
2. *Ibid.,* 13.
3. Some of us here in the retirement community where I now live revise the prayer slightly: "Jesus Christ, Son of God, Have mercy on me, a senior." AMEN

Chapter 1: To and through Pinopolis

1. A funny coincidence: seventy years later I found out that my friend and colleague Jack Spong also fell in love with that place and takes his vacations there.
2. This is the area described by Edward Ball in *Slaves in the Family* (New York: Farrar Straus & Giroux, 1998).
3. See Norman Sinkler Walsh's *Plantations, Pineland Villages, Pinopolis, and Its People,* (Virginia Beach, VA: Donning Company Publishers. 2006). Walsh was a young person in the parish when I served there.

Chapter 2: From Old South to New South

1. The churches of Pinopolis and Chapel Hill are illustrations of what I described in *The Once And Future Church* (Washington: Alban Institute, 1992) as representing churches of Christendom and churches of an "in between" generation, stretching to become the church of the next paradigm.
2. Edward Ball, in *Slaves in the Family,* points to this area as the heart of the slave economy before the Civil War. He notes that two of the major slave-owning families of the area were the Ball and Moultrie families. My first senior warden was named Moultrie Ball. I knew nothing of all this background, and nobody talked about it in the three years I was there. Sanco Rembert, the first African-American bishop of the Reformed Episcopal Church, was born across the lake from Pinopolis in Pineville. I only met him twenty-five years later in a conference I had organized for bishops.
3. At the time John was rector of St. Barnabas Church in Dillon, South Carolina. He was a year ahead of me at seminary.
4. Urban Tigner Holmes III, *The Future Shape of Ministry* (New York: Seabury Press, 1971). Terry became one of my close friends, and I still grieve his early death in 1981.

5. Lewin's work was given to me by teachers from things they'd read or heard. Specific citations are lost in transmission. See also later material about "quasi-stationary equilibrium," another category teachers passed on in earlier days!

6. Ever since then I've had trouble with people who focus on "wellness." Such thinking is around a lot of clergy continuing growth models. For me, the idea of wellness often seems to slip into the therapeutic way of thinking. I want to aim at wholeness rather than wellness.

7. Rolf and Ronnie Lynton became part of my parish and my life in 1960 when they moved to Chapel Hill from Indonesia. Rolf was an organizational consultant who had been leading management training for younger executives in nations across Asia, trying to strengthen the governmental systems in emerging nations. Ronnie was known professionally as Harriet Ronken and was one of the first female faculty members of the Harvard Business School. Both wrote many books. Both advised and helped me for years and became treasured friends.

8. Rolf P. Lynton and Udai Pareek, *Training for Development* (West Hartford, CT: Kumarian Press, 1990)

Chapter 3: Race, Parish, and Community

1. By an interesting coincidence, my father was asked to be chair of a similar committee in his (and my) hometown, Florence, South Carolina. He had far less support for his role than I did.

2. One event helped me define the term "lay ministry." One very hot summer day I had a negotiating session to convene in the second-floor meeting room of the town hall, which was not air conditioned. I honestly did not know how I was going to pull it off—or what to say. That Sunday a church member, George Penick, asked if he could help. I didn't know what to ask for, but he must have picked up my anxiety about how bad that hot room would be for negotiating. When I got to the meeting, the stairs were full of people waiting to get in. At the top of the stairs I saw George and his son with several crates of ice-cold drinks, popping the cap off each one and passing it to the people going in. I relaxed, and things went okay.

Chapter 4: Interchurch Relations

1. Phil was a layperson who taught me a lot. I remember his asking me once something like "Loren, why do you do all that special stuff in the crazy, busy time before Christmas? You call it Advent." "Calm down, Phil," I said, "let me tell you the theology for why I do that." "Oh, for God's sake," he came back at me. "Don't do that. I already have more theology than I'm using." I've tried to be more discriminating before dumping theology on people ever since.

2. I later discovered that the masses of writing on the chalkboards around us for that service bore meanings that rattled me further, witnessing to another dimension of what was going on. The writing—mostly various mathematical formulae—had been put up the day before by another group using that classroom, and that meeting had been about how many casualties and deaths would be the result of a nuclear attack! That knowledge, when I learned it, *did* unsettle me no end.

3. To be honest, admitting now to perhaps oversensitivity to political correctness, we started with the name "Triangle Interchurch Task Force"—until we noted the awkwardness of the initials, TIT, and changed to TAT. There's a message there somewhere.

4. As I write and read this in the second term of America's first African-American president, something in me quails at what I say here. I do not mean to discount the extraordinary depths of racism in the soul of America. It is alive and flourishing in many places. But—believe me—there *are* some moments when we can see and hope for what is yet to come.

Chapter 5: Rethinking Mission

1. A momentary interjection: Isn't it interesting that I speak of ESCRU, OMS, Parishfield, and the Detroit Industrial Mission—and there were and would be many more such organizations—while I founded and led the Alban Institute? So *many* groups have had to go outside the ordinary structures to do what they felt called to do. It's worth thinking about.

2. Roof would soon become a major researcher and writer about the sociology of religion, and the author of a number of books, one of which, *Community and Commitment,* grew out of this piece of research and generated key concepts in sociological thought, such as the description of people in a community as either "cosmopolitans" or "locals."

3. Some years later I ran across a serendipitous dimension of this gift. My son, then senior warden of his parish, searched for and found a talented interim pastor, the Rev. Henrique Brown, whom I discovered had spent time as a student living in that student center in Panama before coming to the United States. So it paid off.

4. While in England I had made a point of visiting Simon Phipps at the Leeds Industrial Mission also.

5. The common saying in those days was that when a German theologian sneezed, American theologians came down with pneumonia.

6. Jean Gottman, *Megalopolis, The Urbanized North Eastern Seaboard of the United States* (New York: The Twentieth Century Fund, 1961).

7. The Mass of the Holy Family came out in 1968 after a long, often funny dialogue with the parish. I had kept nudging the parish to try such a thing for so long that it had become a joke. When we had to replace our old organ, and found out it would cost $6,000, my senior warden told me at the vestry meeting, "Loren, do you *know* how many guitars we could buy for $6,000?"

8. At that time in history, many Episcopalians tended to think that "all the people who deserve to be Episcopalian already are. Why bother about the others?"

9. From time to time I will be departing from my narrative to share other stuff you may want to know. I call this an excursus—and I include these bits and pieces to fill in your picture.

Chapter 6: Project Test Pattern

1. I did not know it then, but this was also a first learning. My job required that I move there, yet that meant that my four children also had to move—in June—cutting

them off from all their friends and everything they were familiar with. They were condemned to an unpleasant summer before they could connect with new schools and people and activities. Years later I was to learn that Methodist placement systems did this to the families of Methodist pastors in a massive way—every June. I tried, unsuccessfully, to communicate this hardship to the Methodist leaders I came to know. I think they still do the same thing more than a half-century later.

2. One peculiarity occurred that became an incipient learning, and helped shape the change we would make in the project. We had expected the conference would give the participants skills to begin planning for mission in their parish. Our focus was on the training we had done. We thought that was what mattered. When I called the parishes of the first conference to plan to visit them, I discovered that none of them had done anything we trained them to do. But when I phoned to say I was coming, each place started calling meetings to make plans to tell me about when I got there. In other words, the training we had worked so hard on had no behavioral pay-off. None! On the other hand, the relationship with the project director had pushed them to get off the dime! Seeing that, I decided that the relationship with the outside agent was more important than the content of the training conference. In essence we chose then to double up on the part of the experiment in parishes that seemed to have behavioral pay-off: the presence of the change agent. So we decided to ditch the conference and to send a pair of skilled consultants to each parish instead. We did not give up on bringing training and knowledge to the parish, we decided that on-site consultants did that more effectively than off-site training conferences. Thank God we also decided to make those consultants responsible for being the eyes and ears of the project—to reflect on what actually happened in the parish as the effort went on. Those two choices were critical bits. There was another essential ingredient I'll talk about later—the necessity for the parish to have some skin in the game. This was how we learned. We tried something to see if it would work. If it did not, we tried to figure what had gone wrong. And then we redesigned it and tried again.

Chapter 7: Congregational Life in Technicolor

1. It says something about my attention to detail that the button was incorrect. I thought we had 28 consultants. At the last minute we added 4 for a Washington add-on to the project. So the "Chicago 28" proclaimed on their buttons were really the Chicago 32.

2. Robbie MacFarlane became invaluable to Project Test Pattern. As a staff person of the Evangelism office of the United Presbyterian Church, he had been drawn into the early thinking about this project. He also helped us connect to an effort in several of the denominations to help strengthen congregations through what was called "clustering." Ted Erickson of the national staff of the United Church of Christ led this informal interdenominational effort. That effort eventually faded away, although PTP actively worked with one of the clusters in Hawaii. MacFarlane became one of PTP's Project Associates and served in a number of research efforts.

3. This well-intentioned promise came to be a problem later when one piece I circulated describing a tense issue one congregation faced between a bishop, a cathedral dean, and the consulting team "leaked" outside the research arena. It cost me an anxious trip to "fix" a gaffe and misunderstanding—complicated by the fact that one of the people hurt was a dear friend—and I simply had overlooked how the

church can take data about the dynamics of group and personal interactions as food for "gossip."
4. During the conference we had continual fracases with the management of the continuing education center. One may suggest the level of intensity going on. When a room was put together wrong for the third time, and I could not get a response from the staff, I remember screaming at the managers at the conference center desk, getting to the point of throwing my briefcase at the managers across the desk in the busy lobby, smashing it into the mailboxes on the other side. Those who know me know that is not behavior one expects from me. The bystanders were shaken up, I was embarrassed, but we got better service from then on.
5. We all, later, took comfort in learning of one rejected contract in Ohio, where the consultants, four years later, got a phone call to ask for consultative help. The consultants, by now busy with other things, asked what was wanted. The reply was "Well, several years ago we looked at things, and a couple of consultants put some good questions in front of us, but the time wasn't right. But right then we started asking some different questions. That just kept up, and now we are ready to take on a serious effort. We remembered your name."

Chapter 8: Growing Interest in Congregations

1. James D. Glasse, *Profession: Minister* (Nashville: Abingdon Press, 1968).
2. Keith Ervin took the training, and his story is told as "The Story of First Church" in *New Hope for Congregations* (New York: Seabury Press, 1972). His initiative opened up the concept of consulting during the period between pastors, and our experience though him eventually led us to the concept of the skilled, intentional "interim pastor."

Chapter 9: "Responsible Closure"

1. One outcome of that conference was the book *Patterns for Parish Development*, parts of which were gathered and written at the conference. Edited by Celia Hahn, it was published by Seabury Press in 1974 after the project closed.

Chapter 10: In Media Res

1. As much for them as for us. Many of their loyalists left for Canada, where their anger fermented through the War of 1812. And the American slaves who defected to the English during the war settled, unhappily, in Canada until many emigrated "home" to Africa and Sierra Leone, where they planted the Anglican Church in Africa and founded a new mission reality.
2. In *The Magicians of Main Street: America and its Chambers of Commerce, 1768–1945* (Oakton, VA: John Cruger Press, 2014), Christopher Mead catalogues how, over three centuries, the merchants of this nation reimagined and reorganized local communities within this cultural flow that Edmund Burke described as "insatiable

entrepreneurialism." See Yural Levin, *The Great Debate: Edmund Burke, Thomas Paine, and the Birth of Right and Left* (New York: Basic Books, 2014), 80.

3. The other denominations went about it their own way, with the same nationalizing pressures. Presbyterians consolidated their northern and southern identities and married them, after some debate in Louisville, Kentucky. Lutherans managed to corral three of their splinters in a disastrous and expensive move to Chicago, leaving behind their cousin splinters in Missouri and Wisconsin. Methodists refused to centralize, building their bureaucracy in five different locations, but built it nevertheless.

4. Joseph Bottum, *An Anxious Age: The Post-Protestant Ethic and the Spirit of America.* (New York: Random House, 2014).

Chapter 11: Best Laid Plans

1. The books from the Project Test Pattern work were *The Minister Is Leaving* (New York: Seabury Press, 1974), Celia Hahn's description of the learnings from the "Vacancy Consultation Project," and *Patterns for Parish Development* (New York: Seabury Press, 1974), a collection of essays from our Mobile, Alabama, conference in early 1973.

2. "Done" is the operative word on this. The first was a project that bombed—an effort to identify the process by which a judicatory (diocese, presbytery, or conference) built a support system for congregational life. In spite of having recruited ten judicatories to report on how they did it, none provided data for us. In that project we learned only how ephemeral judicatory promises can be. But it was done. The other project produced a paper, "Spiritual Growth: An Empirical Exploration of Its Meaning, Sources, and Implications," published by the Metropolitan Ecumenical Training Center in Washington. That paper was by Tilden H. Edwards Jr., Loren B. Mead, Parker J. Palmer, and James P. Simmons. That project involved in-depth, structured interviews with a number of laypersons, but the substantial learnings simply got lost in the transition of time. One outcome was a follow-up piece of research by Jean M. Haldane, published as *Religious Pilgrimage* by the Alban Institute later in 1974.

3. Almost immediately I started hearing people accuse me of being a "money-grubber," a name that really hurt until I got used to it. Later, people were more judicious, simply saying that we were "expensive."

4. As I remember it, the only people who regularly charged for services in religious organizations were people like auditors, architects, tradespeople, and the like. In those days, occasionally lawyers would charge churches—although even they usually waived fees. Even doctors and dentists often gave "professional discounts" to clergy and their families. Money was treated as if it were dirty. "Filthy lucre" was what they called it. These practices were eroding with the growth of the population and the economy, but the emotional feelings were still there and still strong if you named a fee.

5. When, as often happened, a speaker was paid an honorarium for an event, the obfuscation involved was sometimes ludicrous. Nothing would be said before, during, or after the event, but someone would slip up to the guest speaker and pass along a sealed envelope with a check inside. This was also the way many wedding or funeral fees were handled. At weddings, it was often the best man who did the duty. A former bishop once told me about his experience as a pastor doing a

wedding for a college friend. Years later, he was in a group celebrating an anniversary of that wedding when someone asked him, "What was the largest honorarium you ever received for a wedding?" He replied, "I think it was $200 in cash. It was years ago." Afterward the man who had been the groom came up to him and said, "Your answer surprised me. I gave my best man $500 in cash to give you for doing my wedding!" There really *was* a conspiracy of silence around money in those days. My having to charge a fee for what I did went in the face of a long and hidden practice in religious institutions. I was meddling with something the churches thought was nasty. Inappropriate!

Chapter 12: Chasing Rabbits

1. I name them "pastors." Forgive me, you who characteristically use a different term. There are good reasons to call them priests, ministers, clergy (-man, -woman, or -person), or something else—what I mean is that person who takes charge, or is given charge, of the leadership of a local religious community.
2. An unexpected problem developed—at least in the Episcopal Church, the idea of using consultants to help the process of calling pastors was adapted by others to the process for calling bishops to dioceses. I questioned the practice, feeling that the "calling of a pastor" had characteristics different from the "election of a bishop." But it happened, and apparently in many cases it helped.
3. John H. Fletcher, *Religious Authenticity of the Clergy: Implications for Theological Education* (Washington: Alban Institute, 1979).
4. Having already shared, unabashedly, the scientific roots of our impeccable research model, I am almost embarrassed to name the method we found totally unworkable. When Roy and I met every week or two to plan our work, we usually had lunch at the Zebra Room, a beer and pizza emporium across from our office. It became our financial model for funding this research to buy at least one $1 lottery ticket each week, the winnings from which were dedicated to research funding. We never hit more than $2.

Chapter 13: In the Interim

1. Felix had retired from a long, productive ministry as rector of St. Alban's Church in Washington and had taken a part-time job (at minimum pension-fund allowed salary) as executive director of the Washington Episcopal Clergy Association (clergy associations were one of the characteristic changes happening across the church during the "professionalization of the clergy" trend). Many clergy associations were forming in many denominations during the 1960s and 1970s. WECA, partly because of Felix Kloman, was one of the more effective.
2. The story of his work in South Dakota after he got the training is to be found in PTP's first book, *New Hope for Congregations* (New York: Seabury Press, 1972). Robbie and I did a field trip to study that piece of work just after Keith and his wife, Marian, finished there.
3. Names are interesting. We had started by calling it the "vacancy" period, belying the real bias we had in our systems toward clericalism. We assumed, from history

I guess, that when the ordained person was not present there was a "vacancy" in ministry, that laypersons were not "real" ministers at all. I thought that was bad enough until I worked a bit with the Anglican churches in England and Australia, and discovered that they called this period the "interregnum."

Chapter 14: Let's Talk about Money

1. I'm lying a little on this one, to protect identities. It was actually a Congregational church in another state. After they got wise advice from another Congregational church I knew near them, they actually rewrote the membership bylaws for their church. They were worried that people from the downtown church would move out to their country church, outnumber the members, and vote to take the endowment downtown. Faithfulness gets complicated around money in churches.
2. I'm not proud to admit that I told that pastor that I felt he had "pissed away" the bulk of the endowment, rather than that he'd done a good job. I never told you I was wise, but I admit I feel guilty about how I handled that one.

Chapter 15: Expanding the Conversation

1. Carl S. Dudley, ed., *Building Effective Ministry: Theory and Practice in the Local Church* (New York: Harper & Row, 1983). The text is available online at http://hirr. hartsem.edu/bookshelf/out_of_print_buildingeffectiveministry.html.
2. Jackson W. Carroll, Carl S. Dudley, and William McKinney, eds., *Handbook for Congregational Studies* (Nashville: Abingdon Press, 1986). The text is available online at http://hirr.hartsem.edu/bookshelf/out_of_print_congstudhndbk.html.
3. James F. Hopewell, *Congregation: Stories and Structures* (Philadelphia: Fortress Press, 1987).

Chapter 16: Silos, and What's Wrong with Silos

1. It is interesting that MacGavran's studies of how institutions grow their membership have been used to understand how political groups also deal with diversity as they try to increase their share of a vote. See Bill Bishop's interesting book, *The Big Sort: Why the Clustering of Like-Minded America Is Tearing Us Apart* (New York: Houghton Mifflin Harcourt, 2008).
2. *Church Membership Statistics, 1970–1980* (Washington: Alban Institute, 1983). This is a report on the research from the Hartford Seminary Foundation and the Alban Institute, Inc.
3. I'm stretching a bit here. The name Gold Bar comes to me because it's so memorable a name, but I think it was not Gold Bar at all, just a small town like Gold Bar. So don't blame them for my anecdote.
4. Speed Leas and Paul Kittlaus, *Church Fights: Managing Conflict in the Local Church* (Philadelphia: Westminster Press, 1973).

5. Speed Leas, *Moving Your Church through Conflict* (Washington: The Alban Institute, 1985).
6. Bethesda, MD: Alban Institute, 1998.

Chapter 17: Organizing the Work: The Alban Institute's Guiding Images

1. James D. Anderson and Dale G. Lake, *From Information to Action: Information Systems and the Use of Knowledge* (Washington: Alban Institute, 1974).
2. In each of these conferences over fifty American religious leaders worked intensively on the concepts being used in the United Kingdom, theories later published in Reed's book, *The Dynamics of Religion* (London: Darton, Longman, and Todd, 1978). Alban secured one thousand copies of the book and sold them in the United States. I served on the staffs of three of the labs before discovering again the fact that while faculties had budgets to cover their costs, Alban did not have funds to cover my own.
3. Edwin H. Friedman, *Generation to Generation: Family Process in Church and Synagogue* (New York: The Guilford Press, 1985).
4. Russell Ackoff, *The Second Industrial Revolution* (Washington: Alban Institute, 1975).
5. These department names may be misleading. They were ways of operating, not organizational entities with staffs and budgets and work plans. Sometimes everybody piled in to work in one department; at other times one or two staff persons did so, depending on what was needed.
6. What I'm talking about takes time. The expert can jump in and out and be gone in a few hours. This is one of the reasons we got into consulting—very few judicatories or seminaries or other agencies can dedicate the time to really get at problems. The emphasis is on fixing things. We found out the hard way that when you have a real blow-up in a parish, it often takes the dedication of an experienced consultant from eight to ten days, full-time, to walk through that valley. And we found that when you do have a real blow-up, people demand that the bishop get somebody in today and have it fixed by tomorrow. You can do that, but it won't stay fixed! When I hired consultants I had in mind that they were actually "adjunct staff" for every judicatory; they were people most judicatories couldn't afford to have on the staff, but they had the expertise to go in, dig out the problem, and have at least the chance to prove that sometimes the places that were once broken can become the strongest places.
7. When I gave the H. Paul Douglass lecture at the fiftieth anniversary joint meeting of the Religious Research Association and the Society for the Scientific Study of Religion, an address that is usually published in the *Journal of Religious Research*, the editors, probably wisely, decided not to publish it and may still be quietly wondering what I was talking about. Our "research" did not fit the usual understandings.
8. Parker Palmer and Elden Jacobson, *Action Research: A New Style of Politics, Education, and Ministry* (New York: Department of Higher Education, National Council of Churches, 1971).
9. Elizabeth Kübler-Ross, trying to understand the dynamics of dying patients and finding no doctors or other specialists who really understood much about it, went directly to people who were living into their own deaths and asked them about it. We came to see that as a good method for exploring an issue the specialists drew a blank on. We used the method for lots of studies.

10. After this research, with the assistance of the Arthur Vining Davis Foundations, we carried out a project we called "Beyond the Boundary." In this one we tried, with more limited success, to go to the judicatories that receive seminary graduates to see what was available or could be done on that side of the boundary to strengthen the pastorates of the new graduates. In general, we found that judicatories' resources are so strapped that they cannot often stay focused on an issue like new graduates for the long run—that is, for more than a very few years at a time. Staffs change, and there are too many fires to put out to train firefighters.

11. Buckle's original story is in his small book: *The House Alongside* (Auckland, NZ: Anglican Diocese of Auckland, 1978).

12. The four types of church growth are described in detail in Loren B. Mead, *More Than Numbers: The Ways Churches Grow* (Washington: Alban Institute, 1993).

13. A simple description of what that might mean can be found in Loren B. Mead, *The Whole Truth about Everything Related to the Church in Twelve Pages (If You Don't Count the Introduction and the Conclusion)* (Washington: Alban Institute, 1988).

14. I later found, thanks to advice from Ian Douglas (later bishop of Connecticut) and many others that this was more comprehensively dealt with by David J. Bosch of South Africa, whose *Transforming Mission: Paradigm Shifts in Theology of Mission* (Maryknoll, NY: Orbis Books, 1991) I wish I had been smart enough to write! Hans Kung covered similar ground, and of course this literature has seen many additions since.

15. The second book, *Transforming Congregations*, is, I think, the best articulation of what we had been trying to do, with the best descriptions of what we learned and how we learned it, along with some of the conference designs I have continued to use and find workable. It also includes a lot of the demographic data about church membership loss that has continued since I wrote it. The third of these books was written to respond to people who had experienced the thinking of the first two and asked, "Why aren't we getting *to* the future church more easily?"

Chapter 18: Operational Theology: A Reprise

1. Most of our work was done in those churches, but we also did work in many evangelical churches, the Catholic Church, and synagogues. The language and the descriptive terms I've used come from the Protestant Mainline world, but we found that many of the dynamics are identical to those in other faith groups—sometimes with different names. We also did substantial work in congregations in other parts of the world. Since leaving Alban, I have spent considerable time with the Overseas Ministries Study Center in New Haven, especially with Andrew Walls, learning about the many other very large issues, other than these, in the world of international church life.

Chapter 19: The Calling We All Have

1. I am using the word "parish" here, but I also mean "congregation." Different religious groups like one word or the other, and there are good reasons for that. "Congregation" puts the emphasis on the people who are members or participants

in a particular local church. "Parish," which I am using, comes out of the usage in Europe and my Episcopal background. It refers to geography and to the total population of that geography (including people who may not associate themselves with that church). But really, the parish includes even more than that—the horses and cattle, the dogs and cats, the fields and woods, the schools and businesses—the whole kit and caboodle. Of course I'm talking *mostly* about the people, but give me a bit of leeway here. It's sort of biblical, like Jonah talking about Nineveh: "And should I not be concerned about Nineveh, that great city, in which there are more than a hundred and twenty thousand persons who do not know their right hand from their left, and also many animals?" (Jonah 4:11).

2. Luke 4:18-19.